The Wiley Event Management Series

Instructor's Manual
To Accompany

Special Events
FIFTH EDITION

The Roots and Wings of Celebration

Dr. Joe Goldblatt, CSEP

BICENTENNIAL
1807
WILEY
2007
BICENTENNIAL

JOHN WILEY & SONS, INC.

Library of Congress Cataloging-in-Publication Data:

ISBN: 978-0-470-13506-8

10   9   8   7   6   5   4   3   2   1

Dedication

The instructor's manual for the fifth edition of Special Events, The Roots and Wings of Celebration is dedicated to the **faculty** throughout the world who generously share their talent and expertise with students. These individuals are responsible for transmitting knowledge to the next generation of special events professionals. They have my eternal gratitude and profound respect for the immeasurable contributions they make in the classroom that advance our profession and simultaneously, student by student, help improve the world and provide hope for the future of the global celebrations community.

Dr. Joe Goldblatt, CSEP
May 15, 2007

Contents

Foreword

As an expert in event management and leadership practices you offer to the next generation of event professionals a plethora of information and experiences acquired beyond textbooks and classrooms. Teaching students in a thoughtful, well organized, creative and academic way can be challenging. As you are about to embark on a personal adventure of teaching event management it will be imperative for you to have an understanding of the critical tools needed to deliver quality content for different learning and communication styles, while at the same time delivering an engaging and enlightening class.

When I am interviewing and selecting potential instructors for our event management program I look for the prospective candidate to have the 3 E's: Expert, Educator, and Entertainer. Your interest in this instructor's manual may be because you have either been selected to teach, in the future, an event management or leadership course soon, or you are intrigued with the possibility of sharing your expertise and transforming that knowledge and skill set to the classroom. What Dr. Joe Goldblatt has done in writing this instructor's manual is take you (the content expert) and provided guidelines of how to take your expertise and break it down step by step into more formal, approved instruction for the adult learner. He gives you steps, tools, and resources to ensure that you will be successful in the classroom as an Expert who thoroughly understands well organized pedagogy. This instructor's manual, through its many examples, outlines, and research data ensures curriculum will be delivered in an understandable and manageable format. The content contained will assist you by providing additional materials and strategies to supplement your lesson planning.

As an educator you need to be able to transition your event experience into tested and proven delivery of curriculum. Dr. Joe Goldblatt's instructional manual provides you with techniques and proven methods to build your own class, beginning with the understanding of student demographics, exercises that will ensure you understand their different learning styles, ice breakers, and group activities that will stimulate dialogue and enhance the learning style, PowerPoint slides, real-life case studies, and effective evaluation tools. It is fortunate to find such a comprehensive instructor's manual that reinforces your personal experience and helps you translate that into successful teaching.

Finally, as educators to adult learners, we are competing for their attention against so many other factors and daily stresses in their lives. It is imperative that as an Expert and Educator you have to be an Entertainer. I know of no other academician that is more entertaining than Dr. Joe Goldblatt. This manual shares the fun and excitement he creates in each of his classrooms though entertaining and engaging games, exercises, and group activities that can be incorporated instructional delivery. You are provided with numerous examples that support each unit, ways to keep students intrigued, curious, and thoroughly enjoying themselves in your classroom while learning a cutting-edge and innovative event management and leadership curriculum. Dr. Joe Goldblatt does this beautifully throughout each section.

I have known Dr. Joe Goldblatt for many years and he continues to amaze me with his forward and innovative thinking has completely shaped the world of event management and leadership education. Once again, he has created another learning tool that will further enhance the classroom experience giving educators the confidence and professionalism needed to deliver event management and leadership curriculums to the next generation of event professionals!

Jodi Waterhouse
Manager, Corporate & Professional Education
University of San Diego

Preface

The fifth edition of Special Events is subtitled "the Roots and Wings of Celebration." I have selected this subtitle to help our students begin to understand the historical context of their contemporary celebrations. Over many years in the classroom, I have discovered that students and even younger faculty are not aware of the origins of their modern celebrations. It is important to grow both strong roots and swift wings to insure the future of a career. Therefore, this edition focuses upon our history and our future as a profession.

How to Benefit from this Guide

This guide is based upon three assumptions. The first assumption, (championed by Harvard professor Howard Gardner) is that everyone learns differently. Gardner identified seven intelligences (defined as multiple intelligences) that enable people to learn more effectively and perhaps more efficiently. Therefore, throughout this guide you will find multiple opportunities to encourage learning in a wide variety of modalities.

The second assumption is that teaching and learning are a partnership and that the learner is the major partner in this relationship. Rather than promote future "sages on stages," it is my goal to develop new "guides on the side". As a teacher of Event Leadership you are, in fact, a facilitator of learning, an educational resource, leader, and yes, guide for the adventure in education.

The term education is derived from the Latin root word "*educare*" which literally means "to extract". As teachers, it is not our job to implant, rather, we must extract what students already know and use this knowledge to better help them understand the critical principles within the body of knowledge identified as Event Management.

The final assumption is that as an Event Leadership educator you are preparing students for partial or full careers within this profession. This guide is not designed to help you merely transmit vague theories. Rather, it is a how-to, on-the-job training, applied guide to develop future professionals. Because the profession of Event Leadership is extremely broad and deep, you may have within your class those who will be content with part time careers in this field as well as those who are seeking full time opportunities. This guide will assist you with preparing these future professionals to accept the life long challenges that promote life long career opportunities in Event Leadership.

Learner-centered teaching provides you as faculty with an opportunity to transfer the majority of the responsibility for learning to your students. I encourage you to require that your students take the lion's share of the responsibility for their learning outcomes. You can do this in a variety of ways:

First, you may seek their input by conducting a pre-learning audit to determine how they best receive information. The millennial generation may receive information through high graphic media stimulation where the baby boomers may still rely on text and illustration. Regardless, it is important to survey your learners and find out how they will best receive the information you are about to facilitate.

Next, you may allow the students some autonomy in their assessment. Ask them through a survey, how they best wish to be assessed. Perhaps it is a paper and pencil test, a learning portfolio, a group presentation, or even a traditional essay or term paper. Regardless, if the student has a vote in the assessment method that you believe is valid and reliable, they are far more likely to do their best to demonstrate for you how much they know and understand.

Ultimately, teaching and learning is a partnership and sacred trust. Therefore, the early work that you do as an instructor or facilitator of learning to forge this partnership; the greater the outcome will be for both teacher and student.

How to Use this Guide to Promote Better Learning

This guide is organized to directly correlate with the chapters in the accompanying text book. Since most semesters contain between 14 and 16 weeks the units or sessions, this guide may be easily integrated within each weekly lesson plan.

However, whether you are teaching a one week intensive course, a three week summer session, a trimester or semester long course, this guide may be easily adopted and adapted to fit your needs. I strongly encourage you to freely adapt the methods and techniques within this guide to best fit your individual teaching style. This guide will provide you with a framework to allow you to become even more creative in your planning and delivery of this curriculum.

Each session uses a multitude of learning modalities to promote retention, comprehension, analysis, practice, and ultimately synthesis. Although every student learns in a different way, there are some generally accepted principles of good teaching practice that promote more efficient learning.

Principles of Adult Learning

After nearly three decades of helping adults learn I have discovered through trial and error that students have at least three basic needs. First, they require the instructor to demonstrate that he or she is organized and prepared. Second, they insist that the material being discussed in the curriculum is relevant to their vocational experience or interest. Third, and perhaps most importantly, your enthusiasm and interest in the subject matter is contagious and adult students are easily exposed and infected or affected by your excitement for teaching the subject you are presenting.

Through careful preparation and organization you will demonstrate to your students that you are respectful of their time and that you are a good time manager (one of the guiding principles of professional Event Managers). I typically prepare between fifteen and twenty minutes additional material or activities to make certain that there is always a little tension in the classroom to make certain that everything is covered within the time frame allotted. When I use PowerPoint slides, I sometimes must delete certain slides to stay on schedule but I am assured of having enough information to fill the time allowed.

I have found that the most powerful six words an instructor can utter to an adult student are "Let me give you an example." Adults bring to the classroom a world of relevant experiences. By sharing your anecdotal experience or those of other Event Managers you are able to create a 180-degree understanding of the theory you are presenting. The second most powerful words you can utter are "Who can give me an example of this?" Often by giving an example and asking for a student's own example or experience, you can quickly frame the theory and link it to a practice that is understandable and relevant.

Finally, after reading thousands of student evaluations of faculty members over many years, I have discovered that faculty may be generally divided into two categories. Interestingly, those faculty members who are the most brilliant do not always receive the highest student ratings. However, those who are both experts in their subject matter and (here is the important part) sincerely enthusiastic about sharing their knowledge with students usually receive consistently high ratings. A wise teacher once told me, "Before students care how much you *know* they must know how much you *care*." Before you show them how much you know, tell them how much you care about their interest in the subject matter and their progress in the course.

What You Must Know About Your Students

Another critical component of adult learning is making certain you take the time to assess the knowledge, skills, abilities, experience, learning, and assessment styles of your students. A study of hundreds of Event Leadership students at The Temple University Executive Certificate program revealed the following useful demographic data.

Figure P-1

Demographic Profile of Temple University Undergraduate Programming and Special Events Students (Academic Credit)	
Gender:	60% female, 40% male.
Age:	18-25
Education:	Little previous event education, 40% of students are transfer students from other schools within the University, community colleges or other universities.
Experience:	High school, church, synagogue, and fraternal or club event coordination experience.
Income:	Many students work part time to support their education and reduce their student loans. Often they work in event related industries such as hospitality, tourism, recreation, or sports.

Figure P-2

Demographic Profile of Temple University Graduate (Masters) Event Leadership Students (Academic Credit)	
Gender:	80% female, 20% male.
Age:	23-35.
Income:	Many work full time while taking graduate classes. Many have some or total responsible for producing events currently.
Experience:	Many have worked for 2-5 years in the event field as meeting planners or event directors in tourism, hospitality, recreation or sports before returning to the University to continue their graduate education.
Income:	Many are earning between $30,000 and $40,000 and are seeking a graduate degree to increase their earnings and advance their career.

Figure P-3

Demographic Profile of Temple University Event Leadership Executive Certificate Students (Continuing Education)	
Gender:	80% female, 20% male.
Age:	25-50.
Education:	The majority of professional event leaders have a bachelor's degree (over 60%) in either business administration, education, theater, psychology, or another field of study. Increasingly, a significant number of event leaders have a graduate degree (over 10%).
Experience:	Three years or more supervisory experience. 50% have significant experience as event leaders and 50% are considering switching careers to work full time in event leadership. Thos who are working in the event leadership field are meeting planners with associations, event directors for non-profits such as the Philadelphia Zoo, event managers at universities, or corporate event managers.
Income:	The median salary for meeting and Event Leaders is $47,000 per year with entry level salaries ranging from $25,000 to $30,000 per year depending upon experience, the responsibilities of the position, and geographic location (market basket) of the hiring organization.

The Psychographic Profile of Your Event Management Students

Although demographic data about your students is valuable, some educators believe the values, attitudes, and lifestyles of those you will be helping learn provides more useful information to promote communication. Too often we make the wrong assumptions based upon general demographic information. We sometimes assume because someone is older they may be less active or more rigid in their thinking when, in fact, studies have proven that older adults may remain physically and mentally active and that rigidity has more to do with values that age. Therefore, it is important to examine both the demographic and psychographic profiles of your students as you prepare to meet them in the classroom. Figure P-4 lists my assumptions of the psychographic characteristics of students and practitioners in the event management field.

Figure P-4

Psychographic Profile of Event Management Students		
Values	**Attitudes**	**Lifestyles**
Philanthropy	Hardworking	Work hard, play hard
Teamwork	Attention to detail	Fashion and style conscious
Creativity	Well organized	Recreation, luxury
Flexibility	Positive thinker	Education through industry meetings
Innovation	Competitor	Learn by doing (on the job training)
Organization	Leader	Adventuresome
Independence	Collaborator	Volunteer
Design	Experimenter	Inventive
Music, dance, art, theater, recreation	Generous	Survivor instinct
Community	Sometimes has difficulty delegating key tasks	Success oriented

As you prepare to meet your students, carefully read the introduction to this guide as it will help you conduct a series of assessments that will confirm or alter many of the assumptions in figures P-1, 2, and 3. The more you know about your students the easier it will be to prepare and deliver your curriculum to help create the learning transformations you have planned and your students deserve.

The joy of teaching and learning is what brought most of us into the classroom. By using this guide and adapting it to your own specific needs I hope you will not only rediscover this excitement but also find new ideas that you can share with your colleagues. To assist you with finding additional resources, as well as sharing your best practices with others, we have created a web site specifically designed for Event Leadership educators and their students. When you visit www.wiley.com/college/goldblatt you will find the following helpful resources:

- Sample syllabi to organize your class lectures and assignments.
- Colorful PowerPoint slides for immediate use to illustrate your upcoming lectures.
- Assessment instruments (tests), lesson plans, and other information.

As you review this guide and begin to implement some of the techniques in your classes it is important to remember that throughout human history teachers have always been listed among the most respected of professionals. This respect is earned through hard work including careful preparation and creative and interesting delivery of your curriculum.

The field of Event Leadership is challenging, exciting, and fun. You are your students are about to embark upon a learning adventure unlike any other. Together you and your students will expand the body of knowledge in this young field. And together, you both will grow as you learn about why people celebrate and how your future discoveries and contributions will improve this profession for future generations.

Thank you for leading this important journey. Your students are lucky that you have accepted the challenge of leading their Event Management learning adventure. And thank you for allowing me to share some of my experiences with you as one colleague seeks to help another to make the teaching-learning more interestingly and enjoyable as well as productive. I look forward to hearing from you after you have tried some of these methods and monitored the reaction from your students. Although no one has developed a single universal system for learning it has been proven that most humans have an infinite ability (and sometimes desire) to learn.

I look forward to hearing about and learning from your successes as we continue this conversation in order to work together to better serve our students and the growing field of leadership studies. Feel free to write me with your ideas, suggestions, or questions at joe.goldblatt@temple.edu.

Sincerely,

Dr. Joe Goldblatt, CSEP
Senior Lecturer and Executive Director for Professional Development and
Strategic Partnerships
School of Tourism & Hospitality Management
Temple University
Philadelphia, Pennsylvania

Acknowledgements

This instructor's guide for the fifth edition of *Special Events, The Roots and Wings of Celebration* was actually the work of many hands. I offer my sincere appreciation and gratitude to those faculty members and industry professionals who served as reviewers for the first and second editions of Special Events. Their collective experience and skill as educators and scholars of event management studies provided me with collective wisdom needed to continually improve this work and develop this guide. Therefore, I am most grateful to Professors Johnny Allen, Richard Aaron, Betsy Barber, Debra Kaye Blair, Glenn Bowdin, Gail Bower, Richard Carbotti, Greg DeShields, Christine Cleaver, Penny Dobson, Donald Getz, Dana Giovinetti, Joseph A. Greenberg, Rob Harris, Donald E. Hawkins, Michael Jackson, Leo Jago, Janet Landey, Dion Magee, Guy Masterman, Jeff Montague, Sandra Morrow, Kathy Nelson, Cath Pearson, Catherine H. Price, Ira Rosen, Rai Shacklock, Ira Shapiro, Patti Shock, Fred Stein, Frank Supovitz, Jodi Waterhouse, Karin Weber, Harith Wickrema, Brunetta Wolfman, and Emma Wood.

In addition to these gifted educators, I also wish to acknowledge my colleagues at John Wiley & Sons: JoAnna Turtletaub, Melissa Oliver, Tzviya Siegman, and Kerstin Nasdeo. Their combined commitment to education in the Event Leadership field is best evidenced through their support for The Wiley Event Management Series, a historic first for this industry. Thanks in large part to their vision and determination, within only seven years over 14 books by luminaries in this field have be published and many have been translated into numerous foreign languages.

Michelle D. Pearl served as the copy editor for the instructor's manual. She is a highly skilled and talented professional whose contributions greatly improved the final manuscript. Her dedication and devotion to help produce Event Leaders is most appreciated by myself as well as our hundreds of students.

Finally, I must also acknowledge and thank the thousands of students on five continents who have joined me in our classroom. Each time I experimented with new curriculum or teaching methods, these students from over 100 different countries, willingly served as my test pilots. Because of their feedback and support, I have been able to introduce many of the innovations that are found within these pages. They are truly the power or "wind" beneath our celebratory wings.

Introduction and Preface to Your First Class

A winning football coach once reminded his players that most football games are won during practice. I received the same advice as I began my long journey through graduate school. A wise Dean once counseled me that "learning requires preparation". Scholars, he suggested, are not unlike athletes, they must first warm up in order to reach their optimum performance as learners.

The purpose of this introduction is to provide you with some simple tools to help your students prepare to learn the valuable lessons you will soon share beginning with chapter one. Years ago when I taught a course entitled "Teaching is a Performing Art" I reminded my students (who were college faculty members) that you must first *warm them up* to *stir them up*. I simply meant that students do not always arrive at your classroom door ready to learn.

Rather, they arrive burdened with the problems of daily life (what should have been done, what must be done) and therefore find it difficult to focus upon the work at hand. By investing a few minutes in a simple set of warm up exercises you may find that the final outcome is significantly improved.

Getting to Know You

The field of Event Leadership largely deals with the rituals and ceremonies of everyday life. The classroom also has many important rituals including taking attendance, collecting assignments, proctoring examinations, and other tasks that have become ritualized over many years. The first important ritual in the classroom should be getting to know one another and feeling comfortable in the group setting. Groups rarely form spontaneously and therefore you must become the catalyst for this crystallization.

I typically begin my course by showing a brief video of fireworks or events (the CNN video of the millennium celebrations around the world entitled "Millennium 2000" is a good one). It may be found through Amazon.com at http://www.amazon.com/CNN-Millennium-2000/dp/B0000488VB/ref=sr_1_2/002-4740170-3911222?ie=UTF8&s=dvd&qid=1178464742&sr=8-2 and is produced by Turner Home Entertainment. I often play the closing scene of the video for a few minutes before the official start time of the class to warm the students up for the learning that will follow.) This accomplishes two important tasks. First the video gives the students something spectacular and exciting to focus upon and put them in the mood for event leadership studies. Second, it creates a sense of wonder (in fact as some students wander into the classroom they think they may be tardy) as the countdown to the start of class begins.

Next, I always start precisely on time. Because you are teaching time management I believe it is critical that you set the example from the very beginning of the proper use of the limited time that is available to you and your students. I often look at the clock and say "Good (afternoon or evening), I am Dr. Goldblatt, this is Event Leadership and I always start precisely on time to honor your commitment to arriving on time. In fact, I not only start on time, but I am so efficient, that sometimes with your help I finish a few minutes early? Do you like that?" At this point the students usually cheer! Then I add, "You see, if we work hard together and use our time efficiently we can save time for family, recreation, and event celebration. How does that sound?" Once again the students smile and often clap their hands.

The point of starting with this type of positive statement is to first encourage them to arrive on time. Sometimes I also add, "My definition of on time in the field of event management is *early.*" Then I ask them to explain what I mean by that statement. They usually explain that in order to be ready to or work they have to be prepared. I then conclude this opening by reminding the students that learning is work and they have to be prepared to learn as well.

If you have students who are perpetually late, you may wish to use a technique I implemented years ago. The first time they are late I encourage the other students to give them a hand, applause, for their arrival. This is often embarrassing to the late student but also wakes up everyone else. The second time they are late, I lock the door and do not admit them. Upon locking the door, I have rarely had a student be late the second time.

Once I have fully captured the students' attention I ask them if they ever have trouble remembering names. They usually nod their heads affirmatively and rapidly in unison. Once more I ask, "Would it be helpful for you to learn how to remember every name in this room in under three minutes?" Before they can agree I explain the simple rules for playing the "Event Management Name Game."

The Event Management Name Game
1. Bring a simple prop to class such as a maraca, beach ball, or baton. I personally use an ancient set of ritual bells from Japanese dance.
2. Show the prop and tell the students that for over five thousand years of recorded human history, human beings have used rituals and ritual objects to celebrate their joys, sorrows, and triumphs.
3. Hand the prop to a student and ask him or her to rise and tell the rest of the class their first name (or the name they prefer to be called). Also ask the student to briefly describe what motivated them to sign up for the course and what they hope to gain from this experience. Finally, tell the first student, that he or she and his and her colleagues must remain standing after they introduce themselves to the rest of the class. Next, tell the other students that after the student says their name they must, as a group, extend their arm toward the student point their index finger directly at him or her while repeating the students name loudly. Some students will find this amusing and you may wish to break the tension by explaining, "I know your mother told you that it is impolite to point, but you can go ahead and blame me. Today, you must point to play."
4. As soon as the first student says their name, you will lead the rest of the students in pointing and saying the student's name and then tell them to follow action this with clapping their hands loudly in a single motion.
5. Repeat this action and keep passing the ritual object until all students have introduced themselves (and make sure they remain standing!). During each introduction make certain you encourage the rest of the students to clap.

Also, after each student introduces him or herself make certain you say. "Welcome". You may find it more interesting to use a wide range of languages to welcome the students. You may refer to chapter one of the accompanying textbook to learn how to express welcome in over 15 different languages. This is also a good opportunity to begin to refer students to their new textbook.

6. Once every student has introduced him or herself ask them to remain standing and to repeat the exercise one more time at twice the pace without passing the ritual object. You may wish to snap your fingers or clap your hands to accelerate and set the pace.

7. When all students have completed this exercise ask the students to recall the names of individual students when you point to them and mention some brief facts that they mentioned earlier during their introduction. For example, you can ask "So, who can tell me the name of this student who is switching her career from advertising to Event Management?" As you do this, you will quickly hear dozens of students shouting the name of the student you have selected.

8. After you do this two or three times commend the students for their ability to recall names, facts, and their overall ability to learn new information in a brief period of time when they are fully concentrating on the task at hand.

9. Encourage them to applaud one another and be seated.

10. Finally, ask the students why they think you have taken a few minutes to have them learn each others names and why you want to know their reason for selecting the course and their goals and objectives as learners. This will provoke a lively discussion that will begin to introduce to the students the importance of turning ordinary experiences (such as a first class meeting) into a extraordinary event (learning every ones name) through a system that makes it easy, simple, and fun.

This entire exercise will require about 15 minutes of class time and will allow you to integrate the late comers (those that are just now finding your classroom) as well as break the ice and let the students get to know one another in a fun and informative manner. At the conclusion of this brief exercise your students should be more engaged and ready to learn.

Another way to encourage interaction among the students and prepare them for learning is to assign them pre-work before the first class. I will send them an email and ask them to bring a ritual object that means something to them concerning a celebration they participated in or attended. The object could be an award they received, a program for a sports event or a concert, a wedding invitation, or even a photo of a favorite event they attended. I then ask a few students to show their object, pass it around, and describe why it is meaningful to them. I conclude this exercise by talking about why events and celebrations are filled with special meanings and how important it is for the event leader to help their stakeholders discover and experience the power that comes from this meaning.

Dr. Joseph A. Greenberg (Professor Emeritus of The George Washington University Graduate School of Education and Human Development) uses a similar technique with adult learners. Joe creates a series of word games and places them on transparencies and then asks the students to solve the puzzle individually or as a group. Sometimes the puzzles are related to the actual subject matter and sometimes they are not. However, each word game engages (captivates) the attention of the learner, improves concentration, strengthens their analytical skills, and when the student is successful in solving the puzzle, boosts their confidence level.

For additional ideas regarding ice breakers or warm up exercises I suggest you refer to Roger Von Oech's book entitled "A Whack in the Side of the Head" (Warner Business Books, 1998) where you will find hundreds of creative exercises and games to quickly improve concentration and thinking skills while having a lot of fun with your students. Yes, learning can be fun and I have found that when students are working hard while having fun they learn best because they are engaged through one of the seven multiple intelligences (linguistic, logical, musical, spatial, bodily, interpersonal, intrapersonal, and naturalist) identified by Howard Gardner.

Setting the Stage

The physical design of the classroom may be used to promote learning. Prior to the arrival of the students, take time to review the physical possibilities of the classroom. Identify where the best and the worst seats are and try to change the seating arrangement so that everyone has a good seat. Refer to Chapter three in the accompanying textbook for specific instructions on how to arrange the seating for maximum comfort and learning opportunities. Once you rearrange the chairs you may later refer the students to Chapter three to let them know that their teacher is actually using the textbook to improve the learning event to benefit your students.

Setting the Agenda

You will notice that every PowerPoint presentation begins with a slide entitled *agenda*. The agenda slide allows your students to know what must be accomplished and how you will do this together. When I introduce this slide I usually immediately ask, "Are you prepared to follow path to hopefully reach our destination?" Sometime the answer is a rapid "yes" and other times the agenda must be slightly modified. Regardless of what the answer is you must be prepared to first let the students know the path you will be leading them by and then make certain they are prepared to travel along side you. If they are not prepared, it is wise to adjust the route at this point to make certain you arrive at the same successful destination.

The agenda typically frames the various activities within the class into fifteen-minute segments. Following is a typical individual session agenda.

Sample Session Agenda and Timing for 50 Minute Class Session	
Part One	
Segment One:	Welcome, ice breaker, learning warm-up (5 minutes).
Segment Two:	Introduction of agenda and acceptance of agenda by students. (2 minutes)
Segment Three:	Review of previous session's material through the use of rhetorical questioning (Example: What are the first and final tasks in the production schedule?"). (3 minutes)
Segment Four:	Chapter/lecture (15 minutes)
Segment Five:	Media (video tape illustrating lecture content) (3 minutes)
Segment Five:	Discussion of lecture (5 minutes)
Part Two	
Segment Six:	Activity to process and apply lecture (10 minutes)
Segment Seven:	Discussion of activity, reports from groups (5 minutes)
Segment Eight:	Assignment for next session, announcements, dismissal (2 minutes)

Note: The times listed above may be adjusted by reducing or expanding the time per segment or dividing the sessions into part one and part two (see above) for courses that meet less frequently for longer sessions.

The agenda provides the spine for you to begin assembling the various appendages that will comprise a robust and active learning adventure for your students. Although you may arrange the agenda in any order you desire to reflect your individual teaching style, two things are critically important. First, always introduce the agenda at the beginning of the session so that the students recognize your organizational ability and are prepared to accompany you during this dynamic journey. Second, be prepared to adjust the agenda-based upon the feedback and input from your students. For example, they may need more time for review or wish to invest more time in discussing a complex theory or controversial idea. Over many years of teaching I have discovered that the best pace for any teacher is to find the tempo that compliments the learning style of the students and then occasionally quicken the tempo or pace to challenge them to keep up and catch up.

Mini lectures

Years ago when I first began teaching at the college level, I filled every minute of the class with dynamic and fascinating guest speakers. My assumption was that with such rich and valuable human resources within the Washington, DC area it would be wise to use them to help the students make career contacts. When I received my first student evaluations I was shocked to read over and over again, "We registered for this course to learn from our instructor. There are too many guest speakers." I quickly changed my course to blend guest speakers as a supporting element to my mini lectures.

A mini lecture is when you present the major content for the chapter or a case student in a brief period of time (usually under twenty minutes). I always illustrate the mini lecture with PowerPoint slides and sometimes use a video clip to further reinforce the key points. For example, if I am lecturing about pyrotechnics I will show a video clip of various pyrotechnic effects to make certain the students both see and hear what I am attempting to transmit.

Education professionals have long known that students retain a small part of what you are saying, they retain more when you add a visual element, and they retain and understand the most when you involve them in an activity to demonstrate the concept you are describing. Therefore, every mini lecture should begin with a description, continue with an illustration, and conclude with a demonstration in which the student must actively participate (discussion, demonstration, and/or practical training).

Media

A wide variety of Event Leadership related video and audio and graphic media is available to support and enhance your lectures. I have found that some of the best video is available through my local video rental store as I use a clip from a current or recent motion picture to illustrate a point. I have used clips from the film "Father of the Bride" (Sandollar Productions, 1991) to illustrate the problems that can occur with a wedding consultant who does not reflect the taste and sensitivity of the stakeholders and the hilarious film "Waiting for Guffman" (Castle Rock Entertainment, 1996) to depict what "not to do" when planning a civic event. Students enjoy seeing contemporary motion pictures as part of the class lesson.

Make certain you always introduce the video clip with a brief description of the plot and explain why you are showing this segment. Next, roll the segment and make sure you select a brief, self-contained moment from the film that does not last more than three minutes. Finally, after the laughter has subsided, take a moment and ask the students what they have learned from this clip. Also make certain that the clip is no longer than three minutes in length to avoid losing the students' interest and distracting from the key points you need to make curing your overall lecture.

I have also had great success with using an audio tape of a luminary in the event field. The George Washington University Event Management and Marketing Archives has dozens of audio interviews with leaders in this field and they will duplicate them for you for a small fee. (www.gwu.edu) The Event Management and Marketing Archives also contains dozens of video tapes ranging from the Olympic Games opening ceremonies to corporate events and the staff will copy them for you for a small fee. You may contact the staff by telephone at (202) 994-1000 and request the Gelman Library Department of Special Collections. You may also review the collection on line at www.gwu.edu and click on Gelman Library and then search the online catalog entitled *Aladin*.

Discussion

Many faculty members choose to award credit for class participation and this is most often evaluated through classroom discussion. However, to ensure that everyone participates I often assign a brief discussion topic to one or more students so they are prepared to discuss this section of the textbook or a reading from a refereed journal or periodical.

To insure that the students adequately prepare for guest speakers, I award one point for asking a question (any question) and two additional points if the question, in my judgment, is thoughtful, incisive, and advances knowledge. This serves two purposes. First, when it is time for the guest speaker to take questions, he or she is amazed (and delighted) when every hand in the room is raised. Second, it serves as a strong incentive for the students to research the guest speaker and prepare excellent questions.

Furthermore, at the graduate level I require each student to deliver two class lectures of 15 minutes each. They are asked to select a chapter from the text book that they find interesting and then provide a comprehensive lecture based upon the text, three other sources, illustrated with PowerPoint, including photos that depict the concepts being discussed.

As you will soon see in the PowerPoint slides, I list the review discussion questions and then post them in advance of each class so that students may arrived prepared to discuss the key topics that support the lecture. After all, it is only through discussion, argument, and debate that the ideas within your course will receive their full illumination.

Debate

At the dawn of the third millennium, I changed my course outline to include a debate related to concepts that could affect event managers in the 21st century. For example, teams of students debated topics such as "Resolved: The Internet will make live events obsolete." Two teams of students (pro and con) conducted the research, rehearsed their presentations, and then presented a lively debate each week. This activity was so successful I have included it now in all of my courses. Below is a description of how to structure your Event Leadership debates.

The Great Event Leadership Debate	
FOR	OPPOSED
1. Opening speaker (5 minutes)	2. Opening speaker (5 minutes)
3. Rebuttal speaker (3 minutes)	4. Rebuttal speaker (3 minutes)
5. Closing speaker (1 minute)	6. Closing speaker (1 minute)

To ensure the success of your debates make certain you select topics that are directly related to the readings in your textbook. Next, instruct the students that they will be graded upon their ability to effectively present their arguments in an empirical, logical, and persuasive manner. Finally, keep a strict time schedule for each debate (use cards with time warnings such as "one minute to close").

At the conclusion of each debate you may wish to open the discussion to the gallery (the rest of the class) for a brief period of open debate. Make certain you enforce the same rules (facts rather than opinions, logical assumptions and arguments, and persuasive arguments). At the conclusion of the debate you may wish to have the entire class vote for the best debaters (using the criteria stated above) as well as score the teams yourself or with the help of colleagues.

In the end, everyone wins because you have required the students to complete additional research, the ideas have been illuminated and expanded through logical argument, and you may have even reached a different conclusion than your earlier assumption. Some students have told me that they purposely elected to argue against a topic they actually supported because it forced them to conduct better research to effectively argue a view that they did not automatically subscribe to. These are usually your best students.

Guest Speakers
Because Event Leadership is still an emerging field and profession, you will greatly benefit from those pioneers and current working professionals who are willing to speak to your students. In every community there is rich abundance of professionals in the Event Leadership industry who may agree to speak to your students. Below are some helpful guidelines to insure that your speakers are appropriate, on time, and on target.

Coordinating Event Leadership Guest Speakers

1. Use the Worldwide Resource Directory of The International Special Events Society (ISES) or the Finder Service at www.ises.com to identify experts in your community.
2. Telephone or email your proposed speaker and invite them to share their expertise with your students. Provide them with the date, time, and topic. Tell them that you will be happy to interview them if they do not feel comfortable presenting a brief presentation.
3. Make certain the topic matches the chapter or session topic so that there is real world relevance with the textbook and other theoretical material. Send a copy of your syllabus or course outline to the speaker in advance (as an e-mail attachment) so they can be sure that their presentation is on target.
4. Send the speaker complete travel information including the route, the parking location, the building address, the classroom number. If possible, offer to provide transportation for the speaker or, at the very least, complimentary parking.
5. Tell the speaker about your students (demographics, experience level, homeland, and other pertinent data that will help them prepare the presentation).
6. Encourage the speaker to use PowerPoint slides or work from a brief outline. Also, invite your speaker to bring a video of their work (such as recent events they have produced) or samples of their work (invitations, time lines, production schedules, renderings of event designs).

7. Give them a strict time frame. I often use an odd number of minutes to make sure I have their attention. Typically I tell speakers they have 17 minutes plus 10 minutes for questions and answers. Some of your speakers will not be effective presenters so by limiting their time you are limiting the damage they can do to the flow of your program. If the speaker appears to be going over time wait for them to pause and then ask, "May we take some questions?"
8. Discuss in advance with your students the nature of the speaker who will be presenting to them and encourage them to prepare questions in advance based upon the reading in your textbook and other sources. Send the students your speaker's web address so they may conduct research about their firm and formulate questions before their guest lecture.
9. Tell the students that you will award .5 points for merely raising their hand and an additional 1 point for exceptionally in-depth and brilliant questions. Make certain you record this in your course syllabus under class participation points. This accomplished two important outcomes. First, the students who are shy or fearful of asking questions are encouraged by a future grade to raise their hand and to try to earn the additional point through a thoughtful questions. Second, and just as important, your guest speaker will see a sea of hands and think, "what a brilliant, engaged, and interested group of students!"
10. Schedule the speaker for the end of the class or just before the break so you have time to let the students visit with him or her individually.
11. Always send a thank you note to the speaker immediately after the presentation. You may also wish to present them with a gift in front of the class. I also ask the speaker for his or her e-mail address and then (after the speaker has departed) request that each student send the speaker a thank you note over the Internet.

Used properly and in moderation, guest speakers can be a major enhancement for your curriculum and will also lead students to the world of work through their interactions with your visitors. I typically use guest speakers three or four times over a fifteen-week semester unless there is a fabulous opportunity (such as a visiting author, celebrity, or topical speaker). Your goal should be to always make certain your speakers stay on topic, on target, and on time. If you do this, the speaker will have a successful experience and your students will greatly benefit.

Field Trips

In addition to guest speakers, I often schedule one or two field trips so that my students may meet event leaders in their home environment. Figure 1 lists some typical locations where you may wish to bring your students to further foster experiential learning.

Figure 1

Field Trip Sample Locations and Activities		
Location	**Activity**	**Assessment**
Trade show or exhibition	Observe set up or show in progress.	Conduct risk assessment, conduct SWOT (strengths, weaknesses, opportunities, and threats) analysis.
Design or Décor studio	Observe props, sets, and discuss creative process	Require that students select props from inventory to decorate an event you suggest.
Hotel	Conduct site inspection with Sales Manager or Director of Catering	Require students to develop a comprehensive site inspection check list based upon the property they have inspected.
Convention Center	Conduct a behind the scenes tour of a convention center.	Require students to identify risks they observed as well as conceptualize how they would produce a public versus a private show in the center.
Theme or Amusement Park or other Attraction	Conduct a behind the scenes tour of a theme or amusement park or other attraction such as the Zoo or Aquarium.	Ask students to conceptualize how they would design events in the facility for a group of children versus senior citizens and then conduct a SWOT analysis of each event.
Sports Event	Conduct a behind the scenes tour of a stadium, arena, or coliseum.	Ask students to describe how they would design an interactive event for corporation holding an event at the facility during a non-game period.
Restaurant Private Dining Room	Conduct a tour of the entire facility including kitchens and then the private dining room.	Ask students to design the menu with the chef for an event at the restaurant and to establish timings to allow for speeches and award presentations.

Concert hall or theater	Conduct a backstage tour of the facility led by the stage manager.	Ask students to describe how they would stage a awards presentation and provide security for the VIP presenters and award recipients. Ask them to describe how they would adapt this event for a television broadcast.
State or county fair	Conduct a tour of a agricultural fair with the fair manager or his or her designee	Ask the students to describe how they would create a "corporate day" for their corporation within the fair and how they would insure that the corporation is well recognized through branding.
Mega event such as the Olympic Games, NFL Super Bowl, World's Fair or other major event	Conduct a comprehensive tour of the event site during set up or during the actual event and then focus upon one specific component such as the media relations area.	Ask the students to identify the goals and objectives for the event and then how they would improve the outcomes of the overall event as well as the specific component they examined.

Comprehensive Assessment: How Do You Know that They Know?

Rather than use solely traditional paper and pencil quizzes or tests (such as multiple choice, true-false) I prefer to use a wide range of assessment tools to ensure that students retain, recall, understand, apply, and synthesize the curriculum I am transmitting.

Therefore, during a typical semester or term I may use a short quiz to test recall, a brief essay that addresses a problem to assess their understanding and analytical capabilities, and a learning portfolio to evaluate their ability to apply the lessons of the course to a practical event case and synthesize their studies into a series of solutions. The level of the students will also determine the most appropriate assessment device. For example, the undergraduate students may be more comfortable with paper and pencil tests whereas the graduate or post-graduate students may find an essay or case study analysis a better way to express their knowledge, comprehension, and problem solving abilities.

It is important that students clearly understand why and how their progress is being assessed. I use a rubric for each assignment that breaks down the components as shown in figure 2 below.

Figure 2

Assignment Rubric

Total points: 15

Purpose of Assessment: To assess your ability to research, observe, analyze, deconstruct, and understand a complex event you have attended.

Event components: Your event must include catering, entertainment, décor, advertising, promotion, public relations, public and or private transportation, and risk management components.

Final Product: 3000 word term paper critiquing an event you have Attended that is supported by no less than five sources from books other than your text book or the Internet. Also acceptable are referred journals, trade and consumer publications and personal communications.

Format: Use APA style guidelines, double space and number all pages. Include a cover sheet with your name, instructors name, course title and number, and title of your paper.

Transmission: Only hard copies will be accepted. Papers must be stapled top left with cover page.

Rubric for Grading:

SWOT analysis: Maximum of 5 points

Research (Quality and Number of Secondary Sources): Maximum of 5 points.

Interviews with two or more event leaders responsible for orchestrating this event: Maximum of 1.5 points.

Analysis and Synthesis of all event components: Maximum of 2.5 points.

Spelling, grammar, and punctuation: 1

Due date: At beginning of class session 8, March 15, 2008.

Ultimately every instructor must ask, "What is it that want them to achieve and how will I know that they have achieved this?" I find that students at every level prefer continuous assessment to benchmark their progress and then a capstone or final project to confirm that they have satisfactorily achieved their goals in the course. Through continuous feedback, you can provide your students with the positive reinforcement and corrections they need to ultimately succeed.

Therefore, I not only use the traditional mid term and final exam methodology for my undergraduate and graduate students, but also require weekly reports, individual meetings with me prior to the submission of the final project, and the use of a wide range of assessments to compute the final grade.

Teaching and learning is a comprehensive process. Your assessment should be equally comprehensive and result in a fair outcome for your students. Figure 3 lists typical assessments for undergraduate, graduate, and continuing education students.

Figure 3

Typical Assessment Techniques for Undergraduate, Graduate, and Continuing Education Students		
Level	Assessment	Guidelines and Rubric
Undergraduate		
	Essay	1000-3000 words. See Figure 2 above for rubric guidelines.
	Weekly quizzes	25 multiple choice questions covering definitions in text book or key concepts covered in lectures. Each quiz may be worth a total of 5 points with each question worth .02 points.
	Mid term	50-75 multiple choice and open ended questions covering material in the text book and key concepts covered in lectures. Mid term may be worth a total of 10 points or .2 to .13333 per question/item.
	Debate	See format described above. Rubric would include points for research (3), persuasive arguments (5), and rebuttal (2) for a total of 10 points.
	Event Leader Oral History Interviews	Interview three or more Event Leaders after you have conducted in-depth research about their career. Ask no less than ten questions about their career development, current work, and future goals. Include one probe such as "Why? How do you know?, Can you tell more about this?" for each question. Submission format should include questions and answers and a reference list of all pre-research. Rubric: Quality of questions: Maximum of 5 points, Quality of Probes: Maximum of 3 points, Spelling, Grammar, and Punctuation: Maximum of 2 points.
	Event Specification Guide	Produce a detailed Event Specification Guide for an event of your choice. Use format as show in your text book. Rubric: Attention to instructions and detail: Maximum of 5 points. Accurate listing of all event components and proper timings: Maximum 3 points. Spelling, grammar, and punctuation: Maximum of 2 points.
	Event Budget	Produce a detailed budget for your event listing all account codes, projected and actual revenue and expenses. Attention to instructions and detail: Maximum of 5 points. Comprehensive listing of all expenses and revenue: Maximum of 3 points. Spelling, grammar, and punctuation: Maximum of 2 points.

	Event Organizational Chart	Produce a comprehensive organizational chart of your event as shown in your text book using Microsoft organizational chart and describe the role and scope of each position. Rubric: Attention to instructions and detail: Maximum of 5 points, Logical sequencing and reporting lines for all positions: Maximum of 2 points, Role and scope for each position: Maximum of 2 points, Spelling, Punctuation, and Grammar: Maximum of 1 point.
	Risk Management Assessment, Analysis, Plan, and Management strategy	Identify all risks associated with your event, analyze each risk in terms of severity and frequency of occurrence, and provide recommendations for avoiding the risk, reducing the risk, or transferring the risk to a third party. Submit in tabular form with 3 columns listing risk, high, moderate, or low risk of occurrence, and management strategies for avoidance, reduction, or transference. Rubric: Identification of risks: Maximum of 5 points, occurrence analysis: Maximum of 2 points, Avoidance, reduction, and transference strategies: Maximum of 2 points, Spelling, punctuation and grammar: Maximum of 1 point.
	Event Critique	Submit a 500 word critical analysis suitable for publication in a consumer or trade publication as a review regarding an event you have attended. The critique should include the components at the event you experienced, the degree of success or failure of each component, the approach of the even organizer and his or her ability to successfully achieve their goals or objectives. Your review should conclude with rating of one * for poor or ***** for spectacular. Rubric: Research and attention to event details: Maximum of 5 points, Creativity of headline and writing style, Maximum of 2 points, logic of star rating to event reviewed, Maximum of 2 points, Spelling, Grammar and Punctuation, Maximum of 1 point.
	Course Capstone Learning Portfolio	Select a theme and location for an event you wish to develop. Include the following elements in a three ring binder that comprehensively describes your event. Each element must be listed under a separate tab. The binder should have a cover page listing the event name, student name, course name and number. A complete table of contents (shown below) must also be included. Each

		section should not exceed three double spaced pages. Components: Cover page; table of contents; section one: overview of the event (why it was selected and what are the goals and objectives); section two: how you conducted research to identify the goals and objectives. Section three: SWOT analysis of the event; Section four: Organizational chart of the event; Section five: Design process for the event development; Section six: Planning process for the event including a complete timeline; Section seven: Finance and budget philosophy and example of budget (revenue and expense with account codes) for the event; Section Eight: Coordination process for the event including how you will anticipate and resolve problems on site and include a complete event specification guide; Section nine: Risk assessment, analysis and management process including a list of all potential risks, your recommendations for avoiding, reducing or transferring risks. A listing of all insurance products that may need to be purchased; Section ten: Evaluation process for the event including your formative and summative procedures for comprehensive evaluation; Section eleven: Your learning outcomes from the event development process; Section twelve: Your career goals and career development plans to achieve those goals; Section thirteen: Your reference list (minimum ten books, articles, or personal communications). Section fourteen: Event appendices including photos, invitations, or other collateral material supporting your event concept. Rubric: Each of the fourteen sections is worth a maximum of 2 points, spelling, grammar, and punctuation is worth a maximum of 2 points and total project is worth a maximum of 30 points.
Graduate		
	Multiple case study analyses	Comprehensively analyze five event case studies and provide a detailed gap analysis, return on investment, return on marketing and recommendations for improving the overall outcomes of each event. Rubric: Research from secondary and primary sources: Maximum of 5 points, Analysis of case and application of research findings to recommendations: Maximum

		of 5 points, References (minimum of five per case) maximum of 3 points, spelling, grammar and punctuation: Maximum of 2 points. Maximum of 15 points per case study.
	Refereed journal article submission	Develop hypotheses and or research questions for a research study and submit an abstract for the instructor's approval. Conduct research using secondary sources and submit final article not to exceed 5000 words. The article may espouse a new theory, develop a new product or service, or provide insight into a current industry problem or future challenge. Rubric: Acceptance of abstract: Maximum of 10 points, Hypotheses and/or research questions: Maximum of 5 points, research methodology and sources: Maximum of 5 points, Findings and recommendations: Maximum of 4 points. Spelling, grammar and punctuation: Maximum of 2 points.
	Comprehensive External Agency Strategic Event Consulting Project	Instructor will select an external agency whose event(s) include potential challenges and opportunities. Consulting teams will meet with agency officials and provide detailed recommendations to reduce challenges and improve opportunities for successful and sustainable outcomes from the event. Final project will be presented first as 15 minute oral presentation supported by PowerPoint and three dimensional props and models. Rubric: Preparation for presentation: Maximum of 5 points, Oral presentation: 3 points, Visual presentation: Maximum of 2 points, validity of recommendations to agencies needs Maximum of 5 points. Second part of the assignment is submission of a written consulting report in a three ring binder. The binder shall have a cover including the name of the agency, the course title and number, the title of the event, and the names of the consulting team members. Each section shall be separated y a tab and all sections preceded by a table of contents. Section one: Overview of the evening including SWOT and GAP analysis. Section two: Strategic mission, vision, goals and objectives f the event organization. Section three: Opportunities for driving future business development through the event. Section four: Human resource plan for the

		event. Section five: Strategic financial and budgetary plan for the event. Section six: Strategic marketing and promotion plan for the event. Section seven: Risk management and safety and security plan for the event. Section eight: Strategic measurement and evaluation plan for the event. Section nine: Listing of fifteen potential local, regional, and national sponsors for the event including contact details. Section ten: Recommendations for future research. Rubric: Each of the ten sections is worth a maximum of 10 points.
Continuing Education		
	End of Unit Case Discussion and Analysis	Event leadership teams will analyze case questions presented by instructor for a specific set of problems associated with an individual event. Rubric: Instructor will observe students and award points for listening, analysis, synthesis, and leadership. Each observable skill is worth a maximum of 5 points.
	End of class quiz	Multiple choice quizzes consisting of 25 questions assessing recall of key terms, mathematical skills, and understanding of analysis and problem solving tools such as SWOT and Gap analysis. Rubric: Each correct answer is worth .4 points for a total of 10 points.
	End of program learning portfolio	Students will select an event in which they may play a significant role in the development and production. Student will submit a three ring binder with a cover page that list the title of the event, sponsoring organization, course name, and student name. A table of contents will precede all sections. Each section shall be listed under a separate tab and shall not exceed five double space pages. Section one: Overview of the event (why it was selected and what the students intends to learn during the portfolio process). Section two: Event research process including five W's, SWOT and GAP analysis. Section three: Recommended organizational structure of the event organization including a comprehensive organizational chart and a description of the role and scope of each position. Section four: Financial and budgetary description of the event including contingency and re-casting plans. Section five: Marketing and

		promotion plan for the event including measurement and evaluation of return on marketing investment. Section six: Risk management analysis, Section seven: Evaluation strategy for the event. Section eight: Final learning outcomes as compared to learning objectives listed in section one. Section nine: Career planning and career advancement strategies, including potential certification programs. Section ten: References (a listing of all text books and other sources used to support your recommendations. Section eleven: Appendices including event collateral material including but not limited to copies of invitations, advertisements, programs, linen samples, photographs of the event. Rubric: Each section is worth a maximum of 3 points.

A Final Thought Before Your First Class Begins

You are leading the exploration in a relatively new field that has its roots in theater and anthropology. This field is comprised of both art and science. Not every teacher is a performing artist and not every performing artist is a scientific researcher. If you recognize you strengths and use them effectively in the classroom your students will greatly benefit. At the same time, if there are areas where you are uncertain or insecure, seek help from colleagues within the industry. You do not need to be a master of every topic in the textbook. Rather you are a guide. As the students guide you can lead them to meet the experts they need to better understand the subject.

However, one of the most essential roles you will play in the classroom and beyond is that of a mentor to your students. Your cumulative experience and knowledge (some describe this as wisdom) will greatly influence the choices your students make in the future. Be careful to temper your opinions with facts and to balance class discussions by encouraging all viewpoints. One of the most important skills a professional event manager must master is that of good judgment. It is also one of the most difficult. Through encouraging discussion, open debate, research, analysis and synthesis you are providing your students with the tools they will need to make wise judgments in the future.

A young professor once asked me, "Why can't I teach every student in the same manner?" He was really asking, "Why does every student learn differently?" As you have discovered, every student does indeed learn differently and it is up to you to ensure that every student has an opportunity to learn and achieve the outcomes you have established for this course. This can be achieved through careful preparation, sensing the changing needs of your students, and your perpetual commitment to improving your presentation skills. Our students deserve nothing less, and the more you recognize this the more likely you will achieve your full potential as a master teacher of event management.

Week One / Chapter One
Welcome to Event Leadership: The Roots and Wings of Celebration

Learning Objectives, Measurable Outcomes

- Understand and appreciate the historic roots of celebration. (see PowerPoint 1.4)
- Link modern events to ancient rituals and traditions (feasting, life cycle events).
- Modern profession and term "special events" emerges at Disneyland in 1954. (see PowerPoint 1.5)
- Recognize and understand the demographic changes affecting global event management growth.
  - Two-income families expand event demand
  - Aging society creates greater demand for life cycle events
  - Multi-cultural society introduces new rituals and ceremonies within traditional events
- Utilize the psychographic changes affecting event length, purpose, and outcomes to improve performance.
  - Events are becoming shorter in duration
  - Event purpose is to create a new experience and transform the guest
- Identify new and emerging career opportunities. (see PowerPoint 1.6)
  - Event risk managers
  - Event volunteer specialists
  - Event Leaders versus event managers
- Understand why education has become the most important factor in event management growth.
  - Complexity of events requires new skills in technology, operations, risk management, and human resource management (see PowerPoint 1.8)
- Identify industry certification programs.
  - Know Certified Special Events Professional (CSEP), Certified Meeting Professional (CMP), Certified Festival Executives (CFE) and others
- Advance your career throughout the twenty-first century.
  - Identify new career opportunities
  - Prepare for your future through planned career development initiatives (see PowerPoint 1.7)

Opening Activity

Ask the students to pair off and interview each other about the most successful and memorable event they have attended. Use the blackboard to list their findings. For example,

EVENT	SUCCESS	MEMORY
Wedding	Attendance	Location
Corporate anniversary	Image improved	Sales increased
Association convention	New sponsors	Improved events

Ask the following questions:

- Are there specific similarities between these events?
- What are the common characteristics of successful events?
- Is the event industry in a period of growth or decline?

<u>Chapter Key Points to Explore</u>
- Events are universally recognized throughout the world as opportunities for communication, education, networking, experience making, and transformation.
- The major paradigm shift in the profession of event management is the universal and global context that has been created through the adoption of the Internet as a major communications tool.
- Technology is one of the major driving forces in twenty-first century event management. Effective event managers harness technologies to work more efficiently and faster.
- Resources such as institutions of higher education, libraries, and the Internet provide Event Managers with unprecedented opportunities to reduce risk through conducting research to minimize and mitigate later problems.
- Every event manager must develop a career plan that includes continuous learning. This can be achieved through self study, industry seminars, higher education, and distance learning through the Internet.
- Use the Internet to establish effective communication between event stakeholders.
- Use on line systems such as Microsoft Outlook to automate event research activities.
- Contact event leadership industry organizations such as the International Special Events Society (www.ises.com), Convention Industry Council (www.conventionindustry.org), Professional Convention Management Association (www.pcma.org) and Meeting Professionals International (www.mpinet.org) to stay abreast of the latest industry trends.
- Discuss the chapter's "Profile in Event Leadership" and identify the qualities Kagwa and Munyonjo bring to the profession and how these qualities compare with the assumptions of your students before reading the chapter.

<u>Learning Connection Answers</u>
Answers may vary; however, this is a guide to follow:

Year one: Identify appropriate training (such as certificate course, industry
               education) and certification credentials (such as the Certified
               Special Events Professional, Certified meeting professional, or
               others) and earn them.
Year three: Obtain entry level position (such as event assistant or coordinator)
               or advancement/promotion (such as event from event assistant to
               event manager).
Year five: Re-certify through appropriate industry organization, re-focus your
               career to use the most recent trends as propellants for your future
               success. Collect the education points you need to re-certify. Read
               The Futurist Magazine to stay current with trends.
Year ten: Review the past nine years and determine if what you are doing is
               enabling you to both earn and living and enjoy your life. Make
               corrections as required make certain these things are in balance.
               Ask yourself if you are satisfied with the quality of your relationships
               and health. If you are dissatisfied, pause, take a sabbatical, reflect,
               and make the changes you need to improve your life.

Week Two / Chapter Two
Models of Global Event Leadership

<u>Learning Objectives, Measurable Outcomes</u>
- Recognize and use the five phases of the modern event management process. (see PowerPoint 2.4)
  - Research
  - Design
  - Planning
  - Coordination
  - Evaluation
- Identify the strengths, weakness, opportunities, and threats of your event.
  - Conduct the SWOT analysis before completing the research phase. (see PowerPoint 2.6)
- Create an accurate blueprint for your event.
  - Refine the accuracy of your blueprint through research
- Conduct a comprehensive needs assessment.
  - Why is this event important and needed?
  - Who are all the stakeholders?
  - When should the event occur and why is this a good time?
  - Where should the event occur and why is this is a good destination and venue for the event?
  - What resources are required for this event and what outcomes are expected?
- Complete a gap analysis for your event.
  - What gaps could prevent you from achieving event success?
- Communicate effectively with event stakeholders.
  - Identify how your stakeholders best receive information and then match their communication style with your methods to practice excellent communications.

<u>Opening Activity</u>

Discuss the best practice example entitled, "Temple University Fox School of Business Musser Awards for Excellence in Leadership" and the case study entitled "Better Follow-up." Ask the students to read the best practice example and the case study in class and then describe how some of these problems could have been avoided through the principles described in chapter two.

Key Questions and Answers (Answers may vary but students should include these key points)
Q: What is the first step?
A: Research. Conduct thorough research of comparable events.
Q: How will you make certain the events us creative but well organized?
A: Conduct a brainstorming session and then connect the creative ideas to the goals and objectives identified in the research phase.

Q: How do you coordinate the event in a flawless manner?
A: Practice excellent communication skills.
Q: How will you know you succeeded?
A: Conduct a comprehensive evaluation of all of the event participants, vendors, guests, and other stakeholders. Use a wide variety of evaluation techniques including surveys, interviews, and focus groups.

Chapter Key Points to Explore
- Research is the most important phase in the Event Leadership process.
- The SWOT analysis enables you to conduct a 180-degree review of the potential event.
- The 5'Ws (why, who, when, where, what) enable you to precisely define the need for the event.
- You must identify every potential gap for the event prior to proceeding with planning.
- Communication is the strong current that guides the effective outcome of all events.
- Discuss the chapter's "Profile in Event Leadership" and identify the relationship between scale and event design as applied by Jean McFaddin to the Macy's Thanksgiving Day Parade.

Learning Connection Answers

Answers may vary, but make sure the answers contain these key points.

Research:
1. Review the event history or comparable events.
2. Interview new attendants.
3. Attend comparable events.
(see PowerPoint 2.5)

Design:
1. Brainstorm with the key informants.
2. Use creativity games to stimulate creative thinking.
3. Link every idea to a goal and objective.
(see PowerPoint 2.7)

Planning:
1. Identify the vision for the event and use the plan to achieve the vision points.
2. The vision should include who will attend, how many, and what they will be doing.
(see PowerPoint 2.8)

Coordination:
1. Operationalize the event by selecting, contracting the vendors and monitoring service delivery.
2. Interview prospective vendors.
3. Create a spread sheet to track vendors.
4. Contract vendors.
(see PowerPoint 2.9)

Evaluation:
1. Thoroughly evaluate the event and the performance of the event manager.
2. Budget for the evaluation process.
3. Design the evaluation process based upon what you wish to learn.
4. Develop the evaluation process to ensure that the results are reliable.
(see PowerPoint 2.10)

Week Three / Chapter Three
Developing and Implementing the Event Plan

Learning Objectives, Measurable Outcomes
- Conduct comprehensive research for your event.
  - Identify the outcomes you desire from this event.
- Identify key sources of information for planning.
  - Contact every potential stakeholder to receive input.
- Design a program creatively.
  - Conduct brainstorming activities to embellish creativity.
- Develop an appropriate theme.
  - Research to develop appropriate themes for your event.
- Establish and manage an effective strategic plan.
  - Develop a mission, vision, and key result areas for your event.
- Develop and manage the timeline for an event.
  - Establish a realistic timeline for your event using history and an accurate estimate of the resources required for success.
  - Insist upon quality rather than expediency.

Opening Activity
Lead a discussion of the various stakeholders that are actively involved in every event. Ask your students the following questions.

1. Where and how do you collect information to plan your event?
2. What comes first, the creative or the research phase? Why is this important?
3. What are some of the typical themes that are used for events and how are themes developed?
4. Why is it important for an event to have a mission and a vision just a successful business must identify this type of focus?
5. Why is time the most important resource the event manager must use to produce a high quality event?

Possible Answers
Answers may vary; however, your students should include these key points:
1. Interview key stakeholders, such as guest, non-attendees, vendors, volunteers, and attendees.
2. The research phase comes first because it helps provide the data that is needed for the creative (design) phase. Research is first because it is used to identify the goals and objectives.
3. Typical themes reflect popular culture (movies, sport events), historical periods (The Wild Wild West, a Toga Party), and Destinations (San Francisco, New York City).
4. Events are business with a brief life span. They must have a specific mission and vision to further define the goals and objectives.

5. Time governs every decision in event management. It is a finite resource. However, through pre-planning and effective organization, time may be used appropriately to achieve the goals and objectives of the event.

Chapter Key Points to Explore
- Explore the visual, auditory, tactile, smell, and taste sensorial responses to create a multi-sensory event experience. (see PowerPoint 3.4)
- Carefully and systematically audit the needs, wants, and desires of your guests.
- Thoroughly calculate the number of square feet/meters required for your guests to be comfortable.
- Invest significant time in designing the registration/reception area. You never have a second chance to make the first impression. (see PowerPoint 3.5)
- Carefully consider alternative seating to improve audience response.
- Explore alternative, creative event sites. (see PowerPoint 3.6)
- Use lower cost display items such as balloons to create large-scale design using a lower investment. (see PowerPoint 3.7)
- Tents may be climatised to create a comfortable temporary room for your event. (see PowerPoint 3.8)
- Select an appropriate and creative theme for your event. (see PowerPoint 3.9)
- Consider the positive and negative impacts upon the environment for your event. Employ techniques for precycling, recycling, reuse, and reduction. (see PowerPoint 3.10)
- Your event requires ESP (event strategic planning). Make certain you are involving the appropriate key informants in the ESP meetings.
- Review the chapter's "Profile in Event Leadership" and discuss the techniques Downey uses to produce a successful festival event.

Learning Connection Answers

1. To identify the key informants for your event, use historical data and interview volunteers, staff, vendors, and others connected to the event to determine who will become key informants. Use experience, special skills, and inclusiveness to select key informants to attend the event.

2. Send a brief vision statement to each of the key informants prior to the first planning meeting and include a copy of the agenda for the meeting with responsibilities for each key informant to complete prior to the meeting.

3. As you facilitate the meeting, make certain you call upon individuals who do not give their opinion. During the meeting pause regularly to make certain that you have the consensus of the group and during breaks and after the meeting speak to individual group members to ensure they are in agreement.

4. Include specific times for each report during the meeting. Allow at least 15 minutes of additional time for discussion. Make certain you check the pre-work submitted by the participants in advance of the meeting to make certain they are on target. Answers may vary, but include these points. First, review pre-work. Second, provide corrections or ask for more information.

5. Make certain the goals and objectives are listed prominently at the top of each agenda and work plan. Discuss with members of the planning team the linkages between the planning process and the goals and objectives. Answers may vary; however, make certain students list precise goals, such as service, revenue, etc. Also make certain they demonstrate how to link the planning process (schedule, team members) to specific goals (time management, inclusiveness/diversity).

Week Four / Chapter Four
Event Leadership Through Human Resource and Time Management

<u>Learning Objectives, Measurable Outcomes</u>
- Identify leadership characteristics in an Event Leader and in yourself. (see PowerPoint 4.4)
    - Demographic
    - Laissez Faire
    - Autocratic
    - Integrity
    - Confidence and Persistence
    - Collaborative Decision Making
    - Problem Solving
    - Communication Skills
    - Vision
- Make critical decisions and act decisively. (see PowerPoint 4.5)
- Solve problems.
    - Anticipate future problems and conflicts and consider potential solutions.
- Overcome communication challenges. (see PowerPoint 4.6)
    - Make certain communications are received.
- Improve human resource management.
    - Promote group interest over self interest.
    - Stress dependability, trust, and collaboration.
- Recruit excellent staff and volunteers.
    - Diversify your staff and volunteers.
- Orient, train, inform, educate, motivate, and inspire staff and volunteers.
    - Provide orientation, detailed training and assessment for staff and volunteers.
    - Reward excellent, high quality performances.
- Create effective organizational charts. (see PowerPoint 4.7)
    - Identify full time, part time, independent contractors, vendors, and volunteers.
    - Flatten the organizational chart.
    - Determine best organization culture (top down, bottom up, dynamic, and cascading).
- Develop policies, procedures, and practices. (see PowerPoint 4.8)
- Improve time management.
- Benefit from diversifying your staff.

<u>Opening Activity</u>

Encourage the students to form groups of 3–4 persons and create an organization chart for an event of their choice. Ask them to follow these simple instructions.

1. List all the potential stakeholders.
2. Decide whether the organization is top down or bottom up, rigid, or fluid.
3. Diagram the positions using a traditional organizational chart template.
4. Discuss where the event manager belongs and why he or she should be in this position.

<u>Possible Answers</u>:
1. Event manager, volunteers, vendors.
2. Top down for a corporation.
3. See example in your textbook (p.113).
4. The event management should be in the middle or top/middle of the chart.

<u>Chapter Key Points to Explore</u>
- People are the reasons events succeed or fail. Invest in your people.
- Careful recruiting of the best staff and volunteers minimizes problems and maximizes opportunities in the future.
- Utilize the resources of colleges and universities to identify qualified part and full time employees.
- The dynamic organization structure is rapidly replacing the traditional organizational structure.
- The top down organization is typically representative of rigid, hierarchical organizations, such as the military, and the bottom up organization is typically representative of not-for-profit volunteer organizations.
- There are typically three styles of leadership. Democratic leaders facilitate discussion. Autocratic leaders direct outcomes. Laissez-Faire leaders monitor the group decision-making process while providing little input.
- Effective event managers (leaders) employ all three styles at various times and for different types of events governed by different time frames.
- The leadership characteristics between traditional and event leaders are similar, however the value system is very different. Integrity is the most important perceived leadership characteristic of event leaders.
- Event leaders must be excellent communicators and confirm receipt of communications, ask questions, and promote open communications among stakeholders.
- Reduce challenges of teamwork by improving communications, reducing self-interest, stressing dependability, focusing upon trust among the team members, and encouraging collaboration.
- Event leadership is neither charisma nor control; instead it is far more complex and requires dedication and time to achieve.

- Develop policies, procedures, and practices to control the positive outcome of your event. Policies justify your decision, procedures explain the process, and practices provide examples of how to implement the policy.
- Review the two "Profiles in Event Leadership" and compare and contrast the skills, experience, and philosophies of a for profit company (McCall) and a not for profit company (Graham) that are profiled.

Learning Connection Answers

1. How many steps up can an employee achieve within and outside of your organization? Show employees and volunteers how they may grow within the organization. Demonstrate how they may move from event coordinator to event manager.

2. Reorganize the chart to promote teamwork and collaboration to continually connect employees to one another and therefore the goals and objectives of the event. Demonstrate how to collapse of flatten the chart.

3. Develop cross training for logical skills such as ushering and box office, marketing and sales, operations and logistics. When training your staff, make certain they learn multiple skills that require successful multitasking. Use dotted lines to depict cross-functional roles.

4. Look for logical and practical ways to form teams within your organization. Encourage team members to make recommendations for forming teams and then allow them to pilot test these relationships to encourage collaboration and innovation. Refer to the organizational chart in your textbook for examples.

Week Five/ Chapter Five
Financial Administration

<u>Learning Objectives, Measurable Outcomes</u>
- Understand basic event management financial and accounting terminology.
  - Budget, balance sheet, profit and loss statement, income report, account codes, loss leader, break-even, profit, gross and net profit should be familiar concepts and terms. (see PowerPoint 5.4)
- Maintain event financial records.
  - You have a fiduciary, legal, and ethical to maintain accurate financial records.
  - Use software to create efficiencies and improve the speed for this task.
- Understand and interpret the event balance sheet and income statement.
  - The balance sheet provides you with an overall picture of the health of your event or event business and the income statement provides you with a snapshot of the event during a specified period of time.
- Calculate the break-even point and profit margin for your event.
  - Use event history and forecasting to determine the break-event point. Use the fixed overhead calculation to determine the final margin of profit desired for the event. (see PowerPoint 5.5)
- Forecast projected revenues and expenses for your event.
  - Use history, comparable events, and macro and micro economic data to project the potential revenue and expenses for your event.
- Estimate reliable budget goals for your event.
  - Determine if your goal is to lose money (invest in the event), break-even, or generate a specified excess revenue over all expenses.
- Plan and allocate your event budget.
  - Involve key stakeholders in developing and allocating your event budget. Seek professional counsel from a certified professional accountant to finalize the budget.

<u>Opening Activity</u>
Instruct your students to form groups of four persons. Within each group one student will portray the accountant while the other students will portray the not-for-profit event chairman, the volunteer treasurer, and a board member. Encourage the students to have a brief discussion about finalizing the budget for their festival. Make certain that each member of the budget team has a different point of view. The accountant is concerned about accuracy and providing the IRS with evidence that the organization is not in violation of the not-for-profit tax-exempt code. The chairman wants to make as much net profit (excess income) as possible. The treasurer wants to cut the budget by at least 25% to reduce risk. Finally, the board member wants to find additional sponsors. Discuss with your students why these issues are important and how proper financial administration can help review some of these problems.

Chapter Key Points to Explore

- Know the financial history of the event for at least three years. When there is no history, explore comparable events.
- Monitor the general and local economy to identify threats and opportunities for attracting financial support for your event.
- Determine what is a reasonable projected income for your event. Explore all potential income sources for your event.
- Identify and confirm all potential expenses associated with your event.
- Use account codes to track income and expense.
- Retain a professional accountant to ensure your budget and financial administration policies conform to accepted accounting practices.
- Use accounting software to create efficiency and accelerate financial processes.
- Profit is the direct result of control of fixed and variable expenses.
- The difference between net profit and gross profit is the percentage of fixed overhead assigned to the event.
- Maintain good cash flow by improving your collection of accounts receivable and negotiating the best terms for accounts payable. (see PowerPoint 5.6)
- Be sensitive to foreign exchange rates, market conditions, and government policies that may adversely affect the financial outcome of your event. (see PowerPoint 5.7)
- Discuss the Profile in Event Leadership and discuss how financial management as described by Supovitz is critical to events such as the NFL Super Bowl Half Time Spectacular.

Learning Connection Answers

Assumptions:

Income:	$10,000 (minimum)
Expense:	$7,000 (fixed and variable based upon 100 guests)
Gross profit:	$3,000
% of overhead:	$1,500
Net profit:	$1,500

Income:	$20,000 (mid range, break-even)
Expense:	$11,000 (fixed and variable based upon 200 guests)
Gross profit:	$9,000
% of overhead:	$3,500
Net profit:	$5,000

Income:	$30,000 (maximum)
Expense:	$15,000
Gross profit:	$15,000
% of overhead:	$5,000
Net profit:	$10,000

Note: The percentage of overhead increases slightly to accommodate for the increased income (credit card transaction fees, additional pre-event labor, possibly additional insurance fees).

Week Six / Chapter Six
Managing Vendor Contracts

<u>Learning Objectives, Measurable Outcomes</u>

- Develop and implement the design for your event.
  - Match event design to goals and objectives of event strategic plan
  - Develop appropriate resources. (see PowerPoint 6.4)
  - Create request for proposal (RFP)
  - Source appropriate vendors (see PowerPoint 6.5)
- Coordinate catering operations. (see PowerPoint 6.6)
  - Assign suitable location for catering operations
  - Determine rental equipment needs
  - Provide appropriate utilities
  - Identify and monitor time constraints
  - Determine appropriate service style
- Use trends in event catering.
  - Incorporate creative catering options such as living buffet and human buffet table (see PowerPoint 6.7)
  - Incorporate healthy food options
  - Monitor changing tastes in alcohol (beer to martinis, wine to champagne)
  - Caterers as Event Leaders (see PowerPoint 6.8)
- Coordinate technical resources, including audio visual, lighting, sound, and special effects. (see PowerPoint 6.9)
  - First determine *why* to then determine *what* resources are needed
- Conduct and analyze the site inspection. (see PowerPoint 6.10)
  - Prepare detailed site inspection check list
  - Prepare detailed function room diagrams
- Develop and construct the production schedule (event specification guide).
- Anticipate and resolve operational conflicts.

<u>Opening Activity</u>

Ask the students to list those men or women who are generally recognized as leaders and determine if they would have been good event managers. Encourage the students to list the characteristics of leadership in general and of event managers in particular. These characteristics may include integrity, communication ability, persistence, collaboration, and facilitation skills.

Chapter Key Points to Explore

- Event managers work with dozens of suppliers and vendors.
- Event managers must review, select, contract, and evaluate their vendors.
- Catering is an essential resource for most events.
- Incorporate creativity to stretch the budget and develop a memorable experience.
- When selecting the best caterer make certain the firm has had experience with events similar in size and scope and style to the one you are proposing.
- Why=what when designing and selecting the technical elements for your event.
- You must develop a site inspection checklist for your event.
- Develop a site diagram for your event and make certain it includes all of the physical assets of the venue and event.
- Determine the production schedule based upon history or comparable events.
- The first and last tasks in the production schedule include inspecting and re-inspecting the venue.
- Allow sufficient extra time in the production schedule to handle last minute changes or substitutions.
- Discuss the chapter's Profile in Event Leadership and discuss what today's Event Leaders can learn from Mary Jordan's eight rules and why she was a trail blazer for minorities African Americans and women in the early days of the event industry.

Learning Connection Answers

- Visit www.conventionindustry.org and use the template for the Event specification Guide to detail the arrangements for a convention and exhibition.

Week Seven / Chapter Seven
On-Site Event Production

Learning Objectives, Measurable Outcomes
- Understand the differences between the timeline, production schedule, resume, and Event Specification Guide (ESG). (see PowerPoint 7.4)
  - Identify key informants and seek their input in developing these tools (see PowerPoint 7.5)
- Develop and implement event contingency plans
  - Make certain you have redundant equipment and systems.
- Monitor each element of an event during event operations.
- Establish and management efficient registration operations.
  - Identify appropriate location and queuing systems for registration
- Coordinate industry and professional speakers.
  - Identify appropriate sources for speakers
  - Develop and disseminate speaker pre-event briefing materials
- Identify and utilize appropriate amenities.
- Identify, create, and post informative signs.
  - Consider placement of signs to insure maximum viewing
  - Consider using universal symbols and icons to promote multicultural communications

<u>Opening Activity</u>

Ask your students to read the Best Practice in Event Global Impacts entitled, "Opening and Closing Ceremonies of the 2004 Summer Olympic Games in Athens, Greece, produced by Jack Morton Worldwide" and the case study entitled, "Trials of the Trade Show" and then construct a production schedule to overcome the challenges identified in the Best Practice and the case study.

Answers may vary; however, the following key points should be included:

"Trials of the Trade Show" Production Schedule

Task	Start Time	Stop Time	Details	Person(s) Responsible	Notes
Inspect venue	7 am	8 am		Event manager	
Decoration arrives	8 am	12 pm		Event coordinator	
Exhibitions A-K arrive/setup	1 pm	3 pm		Event coordinator	
Exhibitions L-Z arrive/setup	3:30 pm	5:30 pm		Event coordinator	
Final inspection	6 pm	6:30 pm		Event manager	
Doors open	7 pm			Event manager/security	
Crowd flow inspection	8 pm			Event manager/security	
Close doors	10 pm			Event manager/security	
Move out	10:15 pm	11:15 pm		Event coordinator	
Re-inspect venues	11:30 pm	12 am		Event manager	

<u>Chapter Key Points to Explore</u>

- Event resources include people, time, money, technology, and physical assets. (see PowerPoint 7.6)
- The goal of event coordination is to improve overall event performance onsite during the event.
- As a result of improving event performance you should also simultaneously improve the financial performance of the event budget.
- Use key informants including key staff and suppliers to develop the production schedule. (see PowerPoint 7.7)
- Make certain you monitor the schedule and adjust where required.
- The major difference between the production schedule and the résumé is the level of detain that is included in the résumé.
- When considering catering management for your event, the location of the caterer is a critical consideration.

- A wide range of audiovisual products is available to assist you. Select the appropriate audiovisual elements based upon your assessment of the size and type of audience as well as the goal and objective of the event. (see PowerPoint 7.8)
- Lighting is a critical element in most events. Consider a wide variety of lighting options for your event but focus upon safety and security and the comfort level for your guests. (see PowerPoint 7.9)
- Reduce audiovisual and lighting/sound costs by saving on labor or sharing equipment with another organization meeting in the same room on the same day at a different time. (see PowerPoint 7.10)
- Special effects should be well integrated to support, focus, or punctuate your event's message. Always incorporate the highest degree of safety when using special effects and post notices in programs, signs on doors, alerting guests of special effects that are being used. (see PowerPoint 7.11)
- When using video magnification, incorporate on stage screens in the on stage live event. Do not allow video production to distract from the live event experience, rather it should enhance it. (see PowerPoint 7.12)
- Music and entertainment can greatly enhance your event. Use music to establish mood, atmosphere, animate your guests, and create meaningful transitions. (see PowerPoint 7.13)
- Provide a professional environment for professional as well as amateur performers in order that they may perform optimally for your guests. (see PowerPoint 7.15)
- Make certain you obtain essential music licensing agreements for your events. (see PowerPoint 7.14)
- From video teleconferencing to virtual reality, consider using a wide range of communications media to inform and inspire your guests.
- You must determine if your guests need, want, and desire tour programs.
- Determine the most appropriate type of tour (cultural, educational, historical, technical, etc.)
- An event within an event is not necessarily an auxiliary activity. For example, the exhibition at a convention may be the major financial source for the education programs.
- Accompanying persons programs may include any individual invited by the delegate (officially registered guest) to attend the event.
- Survey the needs of your guests in advance to make certain you can provide for them upon arrival at your event.
- Review the chapter's "Profile in Event Leadership" and discuss how George "Boom Boom" Zambelli contributed to the evolution of the modern pyrotechnic industry.

Learning Connection Answers

Task and Count	Date and Time	Responsible person	Set Up	Personnel	Catering
Opening reception for 500 persons	5pm-7pm June 1, 2008	JG	See attached diagram, two bars, one double buffet, four carving stations, one coffee station	10 servers, one banquet manager, two ticket takers	See Banquet Event Order (BEO)attached.
Welcome remarks	5:45pm	MD	16' by 16' stage with standing lectern and microphone	Association president	
End of remarks	6:00pm	MD			
Close Bars	6:45pm			Banquet manager	

Week Eight / Chapter Eight
Advertising, Public Relations, Promotions, and Sponsorship

- Conduct event marketing research.
    - Determine target market
- Develop an integrated marketing program.
    - Incorporate viral marketing, Internet marketing, traditional advertising, and promotions
- Use the five P's of event marketing.
    - Utilize product, price, promotion, public relations, and place to promote sales (see PowerPoint 8.4)
- Incorporate both internal and external marketing programs.
    - Market to your internal as well as external customers
- Develop retail marketing events.
    - Coordinate with retail stores and retail shopping centers to promote your event
- Promote fairs and festivals.
    - Determine cooperative marketing strategies with sponsors
- Launch new products.
    - Identify purpose of product launch and develop event to satisfy corporate goals and objectives
- Develop, design, and execute print, electronic, and other advertising programs.
- Develop comprehensive public relations programs.
- Organize street promotions and creative stunts.
- Develop and manage effective sponsorship programs. (see PowerPoint 8.8)
- Create and conduct successful cause/event-related marketing programs.
- Integrate the Internet into the event marketing strategy. (see PowerPoint 8.9)
- Comprehensively evaluate event marketing programs and measure return on event (ROE).

<u>Opening Activity</u>

Ask your students to read the Best Practice in Event Innovation entitled "The Fiftieth Anniversary Professional Convention Management Association Annual Meeting in Philadelphia, Pennsylvania" and the case study entitled "Preparation Anyone?" and then discuss why on-site management is critically important to ensure the successful outcome of your event.

Although answers may vary, students should include these key points:

- The production schedule in the case study was not sufficient for the elements in the event. There was not sufficient time provided to set up the tent, tables, chairs, and other equipment.
- The food preparation was poorly planned and supervised. Hire sufficient and skilled staff for this function.
- Pre-plan for guests with disabilities to be able to accommodate all guests.
- Hire a tent specialist to supervise the erection of the tent.
- Set an official ending time for the event and stop serving one half hour before the end of the event. Also, begin clearing dishes 15 minutes before the end of the event.

<u>Chapter Key Points to Explore</u>

- Product is the event itself. The event product is often invisible until the first guest arrives.
- Promotion includes advertising (print and electronic) as well as non-traditional promotions (parades, stunts) to continually promote interest in and attendance at your event.
- Price is the value proposition for the guest who will potentially attend your event. According to Harvard economists Pine and Gilmore, in today's economy, you are what you charge for (Pine and Gilmore, 2000). To increase the value proposition, layer the event with experiences and perceived transformations.
- Public Relations is what others appear to say about your event. It is perceived by consumers (including event attendees) as more credible than traditional advertising.
- Place is the location of the event as well as the distribution channel for the event ticket sales.
- Events may be marketed both internally and externally. For example, you may conduct an event (a fashion show) to sell retail products (clothing) or you may conduct an event to educate those who are selling the products featured in the fashion show. (see PowerPoint 8.5)
- Traditionally fairs and festivals utilize newspaper, television and increasingly radio to promote their events. Radio allows the greatest level of targeting and is especially useful for musical events.
- Product launch events are complex and require the inputs from the key informants including senior management, communications, advertising, sales, and even human resource management departments.

- Event promotion techniques include advertising schedules, public relations programs, cross promotions with retailers and others, street promotions and stunts. (see PowerPoint 8.6)
- An invitation to a social event is a form of advertising. It must be designed to capture the attention of the viewer/recipient and elicit a quick response. (see PowerPoint 8.7)
- Regardless of what technique you use, you must "extract value with every new thrust" (Westreich).
- Event sponsorship has dramatically increased in the past two decades.
- Every sponsorship program should begin with an assessment of the needs of the event as pertaining to sponsorship dollars.
- Sponsors must be developed before they will buy.
- Be prepared to overcome sponsorship objections. All sponsorships require some negotiation.
- Make certain you carefully service the sponsorship sale to achieve the goals and objectives the sponsor is entitled to and desires.
- Carefully evaluate the sponsorship to demonstrate value to the sponsor.
- Use the Internet to extend your event marketing reach exponentially.
- Discuss chapter's "Profile in Event Leadership" and describe how entertainment strategies as exemplified by David Rich may be enhanced by integrating Event Leadership tactics.

Learning Connection Answers
Answers may vary; however, here are some general guidelines to be used to evaluate your student.

- The marketing plan is the result of extensive marketing research. Your research should include an extensive audit of the competitive market including market basket competitors (events similar to yours) and aspirant competitors (events you aspire to become like).
- Marketing tactics would include advertising (print and electronic), Internet, public relations including public service announcements, video and audio news releases, creative promotions, street promotions, cooperative promotions and advertising with retailers and others, and sponsorship.
- Budget items for your event would include research, writing, design, printing, placement, tracking, analysis, and evaluation.
- Demonstrate with a one year lead time how you would research, design, plan, coordinate, and evaluate the marketing for your event.
- Determine how you will use services, such as "Burrelles," to track your media placement.
- Describe how you would use celebrities, stunts, and the Internet to creatively reach your target market in an appropriate and effective manner.

Week Nine / Chapter Nine
Online and Consumer Generated Media

Learning Objectives, Measurable Outcomes
- Understand the role and scope of the emerging Internet marketplace.
  - The Internet can help build and extend the event brand
    - Build and extend brands
    - Eliminate costs
    - Interactive and secure environment
    - FAQs provide easy access to common questions
    - Acquire valuable marketing research
    - Publish information via the Web
- Differentiate the major advantages of online marketing.
  - Brand building, direct marketing, online sales, market research, product or service development and testing, and customer support are examples of the advantages of online marketing (see PowerPoint 9.4)
- Maximize your Web marketing opportunities.
- Determine the major types of Web sites and their characteristics.
  - Brochureware, show-biz, and utilitarian are three examples of types of web sites for events
- Identify, prevent, and correct common mistakes in Web site management.
- Include security and confidentiality for your Web site.
- Incorporate special features for your Web site.
- Develop and effectively utilize Blogs and Podcasts.
- Mobile phone marketing will be the next media to be used by event marketers.
- RFID technology may be used to better target and track event guests. (see PowerPoint 9.5)
- Measure and evaluate the data collected through your online marketing activities.
- Determine the needs, wants, desires of your guests and arrange appropriate tours programs.
- Develop special events within events.
  - Identify the social, educational, networking opportunities within your events and fully exploit these activities to satiate the needs of your guests
- Organize and conduct accompanying persons programs.
  - Develop appropriate programs to attract accompanying persons to your event
- Comply with the Americans with Disabilities Act.
  - Ensure that your event is equally accessible to every guest regardless of physical, mental, or other disabilities

<u>Opening Activity</u>

Lead a discussion with your students focusing upon the question "Are tours, accompanying persons, and accessibility to your event a after thought or should they be an integral part of the research, design, and planning phases?" Although answers may vary, make sure your students include these key points.

- Tours, accompanying persons, and accessibility should be part of the research, design, and planning phases themselves.
- The research phase should include a thorough needs assessment to identify the needs of all guests.
- The design phase should incorporate brainstorming to creatively identify how all guests may benefit from the event.
- The planning phase should examine every potential aspect related to tours, accompanying person programs, and accessibility. Experts should be used to assist with the planning.
- These issues must <u>never </u>be afterthoughts. They must always be forethoughts.

<u>Chapter Key Points to Explore</u>

- Discuss the evolution of consumer generate media and Blogs, Podcasts, and Wikis.
- Discuss the difference between brochureware, show biz and utilitarian web site design.
- Compare and discuss different event organization web sites in terms of their effectiveness.
- Discuss the importance of security for web site financial transactions and how this is achieved.
- Discuss the chapter's "Profile in Event Leadership" and describe how Boshnakova uses events in Bulgaria to market products and services.

<u>Learning Connection Answers</u>
Answers may vary; however, here are some sample answers that you should expect from your students.

- www.mpinet.org, www.ises.com, www.ifea.com, www.site.org, www.asaenet.org, www.iaem.org, www.cic.org, www.accedi-org.
- Review event blogs (www.mimegasite.com)and have students establish a blog by using Facebook, My Space or another blogging site.
- Record and upload a three minute pod cast that provides pre-invent instructions for volunteers. Download the pod cast to a MP3 player and demonstrate at the next class session.

Week Ten / Chapter Ten
Risk Management: Legal and Financial Safeguards

Learning Objectives, Measurable Outcomes

- Recognize and comply with standard and customary event regulations and procedures.
    - Fire, occupancy, music, and alcohol regulations must be researched and complied with
- Read, understand, and evaluate legal event documents.
    - Client agreements, hotel contracts, informed consent, waivers, and other legal documents must be clearly understood and consistently utilized
- Understand and comply with the general requirements of U.S. regulations related to the Sarbanes-Oxley Act.
    - Determine why the act is important and how to comply with its requirements if you are a public corporation or representing a public corporation (see PowerPoint 10.4)
- Assess, analyze, plan, manage, and control potential event liabilities.
    - Conduct a comprehensive risk assessment, determine frequency and severity of potential risks based upon history, and control potential event risks
- Obtain necessary permits and licenses to operate events. (see PowerPoint 10.8)
    - Licenses such as alcohol, music, street closure, and others must be obtained to comply with local, state, and federal ordinances (see PowerPoint 10.5)
- Develop and manage risk management procedures. (see PowerPoint 10.9)

Opening Activity

Read the case study entitled "Political Campaign on a Shoe String (p. 368)" and discuss with your students how the principles of event marketing espoused in this chapter could have improved the return on event (ROE) for the candidate.

Answers may vary; however, the students should include these key points:

- The candidate's staff could have conducted surveys or focus panel research to determine the approval quotient of the voters. This continuous polling of voters could help the candidate refine his event marketing strategy.
- The candidate's staff could review the instant polling data from each event and determine which demographic group was positively affected by the event activities and message.
- The candidate's staff could review news coverage of the events and a assign a dollar value for this publicity as match the demographic of the media to the surveys and polling data to determine if these are correlative.

Chapter Key Points to Explore

- Discuss the reasons why the Sarbanes/Oxley act was created and its importance for public corporations.
- Discuss the importance of a risk assessment meeting and how to conduct this activity to avoid, reduce, or transfer future risks at your event.
- Describe the difference and similarities between ethics, morals and laws.
- Describe the four parts of a contract and why each is important. (see PowerPoint 10.6)
- Describe the additional requirements for event contracts such as cancellation, attrition, force majeure, and other critical elements. (see PowerPoint 10.7)
- Explore how and why to conduct a safety meeting for your vendors, volunteers and staff.
- Describe the different types of insurance products needed for your event.
- Discuss insurance exclusions and the concept of additional insured and certificate of insurance.
- Discuss the chapter's "Profile in Event Leadership" and describe how April Harris' career contributions have advanced the field of Event Leadership in higher education and beyond.

Learning Connection Answers

Answers may vary; however, these key points should be included:

- Examine incident reports and National Weather Service data history.
- Establish written protocols for determining when to evacuate including a chain of command, written live and recorded announcements, incorporation of sirens and other communications tools and establishment of a rally point for evacuees.
- Describe comprehensive general liability, fire, host liability, workmen's compensation, and other types of insurance.
- Describe how you will comply with the Sarbanes-Oxley act by requiring full disclosure and dual auditing verification procedures.

Week Eleven / Chapter Eleven
Inclusivity, Morality, Law, and Ethics in Event Management

- Develop special events within events to satisfy the needs of all guests and perhaps increase attendance.
    - Promote diversity and inclusivity by incorporating various elements into your event that satisfy the needs of all audience members
- Organize and conduct appropriate accompanying-persons programs.
    - From golf tournaments to fashion shows, make certain that accompanying-persons also have a fulfilling experience at your event
- Promote principles of inclusiveness throughout your event plan and production.
    - Assess the composition of your board, staff, and volunteers and make certain they represent the interests of your target audience
- Comply with the U.S. Americans with Disabilities Act.
    - Ensure that your guests with different abilities have equal access to all areas of your event
- Understand the difference among morals, laws, and ethics
    - Explore how morals, laws, and ethics are both different and similar
- Identify common ethical problems in the special events industry.
    - Gifts versus bribes, taking credit for others work, and solicitation of clients are just three of numerous ethical problems that Event Leaders must overcome
- Avoid some ethical problems.
    - Avoid ethical problems by first identifying likely issues that may arise and then identifying a brain trust of experts who may advise you before you make a decision
- Establish policies, procedures, and practices for ethical issues.
    - Determine what you must do, how you will do it, and typical scenarios for dealing with ethical problems before, during, and after your event
- Identify and use industry ethical guidelines.
    - Determine who must make the decision for ethical challenges and how it will be made
- Appoint an "ethical brain trust" to guide your ethical decision making.
    - Identify advisors to assist you in making effective ethical decisions

<u>Opening Activity</u>

Lead a discussion during which you ask students to list every possible risk associated with events. Next, list one or two specific events such as a rock and roll concert and a children's festival and discuss the differences in the risk factors for each event.

Answers may vary; however, make certain your students include these key points:

- Possible risks may range from slips and falls to chemical warfare by terrorists. Risks are usually related to people, weather, products, and criminal activity.
- Risks may increase or decrease based upon certain factors. For example, if the temperature is over 90 degrees Fahrenheit, the humidity is 100%, and the event is outdoors with no shelter, the persons over 70 may be at a higher risk than others attending the event. In fact, everyone attending the event may be at risk for heat stroke, sunburn, and dehydration.

<u>Chapter Key Points to Explore</u>

- Understand the differences between morals, laws, and ethics. (see PowerPoint 11.4)
- Identify common ethical problems in the special events industry. (see PowerPoint 11.5)
- Avoid or address ethical problems.
- Establish policies, procedures and practices for dealing with ethical problems.
- Understand that inclusiveness is an ethical responsibility. (see PowerPoint 11.6)
- Identify and use industry ethical guidelines.
- Appoint an ethical brain trust to guide your decision making.
- Arrange and organize activities that include everyone.
- Develop special events within events that satisfy the needs of all guests. (see PowerPoint 11.7)
- Organize and conduct effective spouse and partner programs. (see PowerPoint 11.8)
- Comply with the Americans with Disabilities Act (ADA) to meet or exceed the standard of care associated with this legislation. (see PowerPoint 11.9)
- Demonstrate sensitivity through careful planning for visually, auditorily, and physically challenged guests.
- Discuss the chapter's Profiles in Event Leadership and describe how Columbus and Earls philosophies and skills as Event Leaders are complimentary. Discuss how their events promote inclusivity.

<u>Learning Connection Answers</u>
Answers may vary; however, these are typical answers that students may provide.

- Is this a gift or a bribe? Is their a quid pro quo?
- Is this a care of harassment? Has there been a pattern of this behavior?
- How do you self disclose your exact role in this event?
- Youth: Hygiene and physical fitness activities.
- Young children: A trip to a science museum.
- Heterosexuals: Promote sensitivity to other groups including gay, lesbian, bi-sexual, and transgender lifestyles.
- Gay, lesbian, bi-sexual, and transgender guests: Provide special programming related to health issues reflecting their interests.
- Use talking signs, Braille, infrared hearing assistance, hand rails, ramps, lifts, and other devices to improve accessibility for all guests.
- Create a system for observing and surveying the level of accessibility your event has demonstrated for all potential guests.

Week Twelve / Chapter Twelve
Technology and Modern Event Management

<u>Learning Objectives, Measurable Outcomes</u>
- Understand the role and scope of emerging technology within the event industry. (see PowerPoint 12.4)
  - Demonstrate how various technologies may positively impact upon the event industry
- Find resources for efficient technological solutions.
  - Identify technological solutions for scheduling, financial administration, design, on line commerce, and other key event systems
- Differentiate data processing systems.
  - Determine the appropriate data processing system for your event organization and individual event
- Apply technological solutions to solve problems.
  - Select and apply proper technology to efficiently solve problems

<u>Opening Activity</u>

Present the following case study and instruct your students to solve the case problem through group discussion. A large association wishes to use e-commerce to market their upcoming conference and exposition. How will they determine whether to do this using existing resources within the organization or to out source these services? How will they measure their return on investment (ROI)? How will they compare the efficiency of outsourcing versus the savings of using internal resources?

Answers will vary; however, it is important that student include these key points:
- The association should first conduct an on-line test with a smaller event, such as a regional session, to measure the ROI.
- The association should compare the conversion costs of direct mail versus on-line marketing.
- The association should survey the membership to determine if they prefer on-line versus direct mail.
- The association must finally assess the cost per thousand (cpm) of marketing on line versus direct mail by coding all registrations (transactions).

<u>Chapter Key Points to Explore</u>
- Batch data processing allows simplicity and greater reliability. The cost is lower for batch data processing, however it does not allow for quick processing of transactions.
- In a real-time processing system, transactions are entered as they occur. These systems are more common for middle-sized event management companies with diverse operations and/or large event management companies.

- Time sharing and service bureaus are cost effective for event organizations that wish to share their time with other organizations. Small and middle-sized event management concerns typically use these systems for payroll and collection of receivables.
- There are basically three types of hardware in the event management industry: online systems, PC systems, and distributed data processing. (see PowerPoint 12.5)
- Online systems require communications devices connected to a computer.
- PC systems are represented by stand-alone computer terminals..
- Distributed data processing systems are usually connected to a mainframe computer located at the headquarters office of an event management company and may be linked to another through a local area network (LAN) or a wide area network (WAN). (see PowerPoint 12.7)
- Every event management organization should examine the feasibility of developing and maintaining a Web site.
- Event web sites should be listed on the major search engines including Google, Dogpile, Altavista, Yahoo, and HotBot.
- The Web site is an excellent research tool where you can collect information about potential clients and guests.
- A database is an important tool and resource for event organizations to track vendors as well as clients. (see PowerPoint 12.6)
- Technology will become much more customized in the twenty-first century.
- One of the most important develops in the event industry is the Wireless Application Protocol (WAP), which allows event managers to transmit information 24/7 anywhere in the world. This technology can rapidly accelerate the exchange of information, the processing of transactions and improve global networking.
- Discuss the chapter's "Profile in Event Leadership" and describe Steven Wood Schmader's three propellants of leadership.

Learning Connection Answers
Answers will vary; however, it is important that student include these key points:

1. Ability to interface with existing internal systems.
2. Ability to interface with external systems (vendors).
3. Online transaction ability.
4. Confidentiality issues.
5. Security issues.
6. Storage requirements.
7. Training requirements and cost.
8. Potential for expandability and upgrades.
9. Service availability from consultants, vendors.
10. Stability issues.

Week Thirteen / Chapter Thirteen
Career Development, Advancement, and Sustainable Success

<u>Learning Objectives, Measurable Outcomes</u>

- Advance your event management career through formal and informal education. (see PowerPoint 13.4)
  - Identify an education path and credentialing process that will continually expand your career options
- Gain more professional experience to build your résumé.
  - Develop internships, externships, practicum, and other work experiences to systematically develop your résumé
- Become a certified special event professional (CSEP).
  - Study and earn the CSEP designation as well as others that relate to your career goals and objectives
- Earn the credentials you need for employment, promotion, and long-term success.
  - Earn educational, industry, and experiential credentials to foster long term development (see PowerPoint 13.6)
- Build both a life and career.
  - Balance career success with personal fulfillment to build a meaningful and satisfactory life (see PowerPoint 13.7)

<u>Opening Activity</u>

Ask each student to list their career goals for the next 3, 5, and 10 years. Then ask each student to list what they are prepared to do to achieve these goals. Conduct a brief discussion about what is required to achieve long term career success in the event management field.

Answers may vary; however, make certain your students include these key points:

Three Years:
- During the early part of your career you must gain experience (internship), education, and credentials (CSEP).
- Join one of two event-related organizations and become active through committee and other volunteer work.

Five Years:
- Continue your education through industry conventions and seminars.
- Contribute to industry magazines and journals.
- Enter industry award competitions
- Prepare for re-certification.

Ten Years:
- Mentor younger, new professionals.
- Review your career path and determine if correction is needed

Long-term Success Secrets
- Continuing education
- Credentials (certification)
- Professional networking
- Visibility through professional associations
- Willingness to help others

<u>Chapter Key Points to Explore</u>
- Education is now a critical requirement for long term career success in the event management industry.
- Within the event management field a body of knowledge has emerged that includes the knowledge domains of administration of events, coordination, marketing, and risk management.
- The majority of event management professionals have an undergraduate degree in business administration.
- A wide variety of educational choices are available including associate, baccalaureate, masters, and certificate programs in event management studies.
- Use an internship or externship to gain practical experience in the field while positioning yourself with an employer for future employment.
- Use a university or college course in event management studies as a means to identify an appropriate internship.

- There are numerous professional certification programs within the event industry. The most recognized and respected is the Certified Special Events Professional (CSEP). However, others include the Certified Meeting Professional (CMP), Certified Exposition Management (CEM), and Certified Festival Executive (CFE) among others. (see PowerPoint 13.5)
- There is not one credential that is most valuable. They are all valuable and you should try and earn as many as possible that logically relate to your career goals and objectives.
- Finding a great job in this field is a combination of timing, persistence, and talent.
- Your challenge and opportunity as a professional event manager is to record, remember, and celebrate the triumphs, joys, and event sorrows of our lives. You are marking the milestones that future generations will long remember and cherish.
- Discuss the chapter's Profile in Event Leadership and describe how Morimoto and Kawamura use ancient rituals to promote new wings for the Japanese events industry.

Learning Connection Answers

Ask each student to exchange their résumé with others and discuss the strengths, weaknesses, opportunities, and threats that each document contains in terms of long term career success. What needs to be added to each résumé to further ensure career success?
What educational credentials are needed? What industry and experiential credentials need to be added? Does the résumé reflect the personal philosophy of the person who has developed it? Will the job that is gained from this résumé provide the student with personal as well as financial fulfillment?

Answers will vary; however, it is important that student include these key points:

- Does the résumé include a career objective that describes the benefits the employer will receive?
- Does the résumé list the type of event, the number of attendees, and the budget?
- Does the résumé include key words, such as marketing, finance, sales, and other key terms?
- Does the résumé use strong active verbs, such as "planned", "organized", "coordinated", "led", and "managed"?
- What salary level would you offer this person?
- What can be done to increase the salary level?

Chapter Fourteen
Best Practices in Event Leadership

Best Practice in Event Advancement: The Temple University Fox School of Business Musser Awards for Excellence in Leadership

Discussion Questions:
1. What was this event first developed?
2. What are the goals and objectives of this event?
3. How is this event used to support other programs within the School?
4. How have the event planners used their creativity to honor the recipients?
5. How does this event represent excellence in leadership?

Best Practice in Event Creativity: Event Solutions Idea Factory

Discussion Questions:
1. What do the spotlight awards honor and who is included in the events industry hall of fame?
2. How is the location of the educational program a boost to exhibitor's traffic?
3. How was the Grammy Awards case study used to promote creativity?
4. What is the cause related activity that is incorporated within the Event Solutions Idea Factory?
5. How does this event represent best practice in event creativity?

Best Practice in Event Innovation: The Fiftieth Anniversary Professional Convention Management Association Annual Meeting in Philadelphia, Pennsylvania

Discussion Questions:
1. Why was Philadelphia selected for the fiftieth annual meeting?
2. How did Meeting Xperiments generate cutting edge educational outcomes?
3. What is Open Space Technology?
4. How did the opening and closing events effectively promote the destination?
5. How does this event represent best practice in event innovation?

Best Practice in Global Impacts: Opening and Closing Ceremonies of the 2004
Summer Olympic Games in Athens, Greece produced by Jack Morton Worldwide

Discussion Questions:
1. How did Morton's philosophy of "leadership is hope" inspire the development of this event?
2. Why did Lois Jacobs follow Bill Morton to help lead international events such as the Olympic Games opening and closing ceremonies?
3. What were some of the challenges and successes of this event?
4. How was technology utilized to tell the story of ancient Greece in a contemporary manner?
5. What were the global impacts of this event?

Best Practice in Sustainability: The Dallas County Community College District
Max and Rosa Goldblatt Endowment Scholarship Awards

Discussion Questions:
1. How and why was this developed?
2. What is the outcome of this event?
3. How is the event conducted?
4. How is this event linked to the persons for whom it is named?
5. How does this event exemplify and demonstrate sustainability?

Chapter Fifteen
Case Studies in Event Leadership

The following are topics that should be covered by students in their answers to case study questions.

Taking a Gamble
- How does the event manager protect the image and corporate brand when producing a corporate product launch?
  - Identify brand and image policies
  - Discuss with client the final image that should be transmitted through the event

- What legal and ethical issues are typically present in corporate product launch events that may not be as critical in other types of events such as social life-cycle events?
  - Union issues (jurisdictional responsibility)
  - Intellectual property, confidentiality of client information

- How does the event manager know to whom to report in the corporation and who to turn when he or she has a question or needs a decision made?
  - Interview the client and ask, "Who can make the final decision about this?"
  - Ask the client if the person who signed the contract can also approve changes during the event

Festival Challenge
- What could the event manager and her assistant have done to effectively market their event to vendors?
  - Conduct better marketing research
  - Ask for small deposits from exhibitors to confirm participation

- What integrative marketing techniques would be most effective for this type of event given the low budget?
  - Seek sponsors to underwrite the event
  - Cross promote the event through individual stores

- Do you think the situation would have been the same if the event manager had more time?
  - Perhaps, although time is a critical factor
  - Time is important but may be overcome through better strategy and more resources

- How could the event manager incorporate cause marketing in this event? Would it have been appropriate?
    - The location of the shopping mall opens a wide range of possibilities including Boyd and Girls Clubs
    - Yes, if an appropriate course can be identified, it is appropriate

- What type of sponsors would have been appropriate for this event?
    - Clothing manufacturers
    - Major chain stores featured in the mall.
    - Bottlers (Coca-Cola, Pepsi)

- What negotiation strategy would you use to negotiate sponsorship for this event?
    - Provide the sponsor wit title sponsorship and exclusivity for the event
    - Allow sponsor to conduct marketing research at the event (product sampling)

Shower Surprises
- Who was the event manager in this event?
    - This event did not have a strong event manager
    - First Alyson, later Carol, ultimately no one

- What type of leadership style did Carol use? Was it successful? Why or why not?
    - Autocratic
    - No, it was not successful
    - Carol acted without consulting others. During the planning phase the appropriate leadership style is democratic

- What policies, procedures, or practices could have eliminated this conflict?
    - The three hostesses should have agreed on a decision-making process when the members of the committee could not reach a consensus
    - The decisions should reflect the desires of the guest of honor

- What would have been some effective ways to motivate Alyson to cooperate more fully with Carol?
    - Jen could have explained to both Carol and Alyson how much she values their friendship and appreciates their working together for her benefit
    - Marcy, who initiated the idea, should have mediated the problem between Carol and Alyson and serves as a counselor to them when crisis arose

Unhappy Tournament

- What should the event manager have done to ensure that both she and the ACA were protected against lawsuits brought by an injured participant?
  - Written policies, procedures, and practices should have been developed in advance
  - Sally should have signed a medical treatment permission form prior to the event

- What forms should the event manager have included in the registration package?
  - Medical history form all pre-existing medical conditions
  - Waiver of liability to protect event sponsor
  - Permission to receive medical treatment

- What specific details should be included in a medical release form?
  - Pre-existing medical conditions
  - Notice of the rights associated with participation in the event
  - Acknowledgement that the event organizer may seek medical treatment for the participant

- How could the event manager prove that she had inspected the equipment and was it an issue in this case?
  - A copy of the equipment maintenance and inspection report should be kept on file
  - The equipment manufacturers warranty should be kept on file

We are Sold Out!

- Ethically, should the association allow unlimited registration to earn more revenue from increased demand, or should it limit registration and focus on the quality of the event?
  - The association should list registration and focus on quality
  - Additional distribution channels (including distance learning) should be explored to satisfy demand

- If the association limits the registration, how should they alert members about the change in procedure?
  - Association publications and the World Wide Web should be used to notify members through e-mail notices
  - Signs at the annual convention registration desk should notify the members about the4 new policy

- When booking a location for the meeting in three years, how can the meetings department predict how large demand for registration will be?
  - Historical data should be carefully analyzed
  - The industry's financial prospectives should be studied
  - The micro and macroeconomic factors should be considered

- What could the association do to allow members to access information from the meeting if they get cut off from registration?
  - Offer a simultaneous web cast of popular sessions, such as the keynote address
  - Offer post-convention audio and videotapes and CD ROMs of popular sessions

Trials of the Trade Show
What should be included in the exhibitors' policies, procedures, and practices and regulations?
  - The use of live or recorded music by exhibitors
  - Advance scheduling by exhibitors for load in or load out
  - Licensing requirements for music

- How do you design the exhibit floor to avoid crowding, gridlock, and other crowd control issues?
  - Create "destinations" by placing popular exhibitors at the far end of the hall
  - Distribute food or beverage and hospitality areas throughout the hall
  - Use entertainment stages to draw attendees to underused areas

- What do you do if an exhibitor violates regulations?
  - First remind them of the written policies and procedures and request their compliance
  - If the problem (violation) persists, you may have to revoke their license to exhibit

- How do you communicate effectively with union workers?
  - Identify the union chair of command (business manager, shop steward, or other supervisor)
  - Review written union regulations, and document any charges in writing

- What are some creative solutions to ensure that buyers visit underutilized areas of an exhibit area?
  - Offer a sweepstakes/prize give away and place the raffle drum in the underutilized area to draw attendees. Conduct the prize drawing in this area several times during the event
  - Use arrival promotions (blimps), costumed characters, music, and entertainment stages in these areas

Cutting the Ribbon and Healing the Community
- How can you determine the public relations challenges for your municipal event and work with your client to mitigate these potential problems?
  - Monitor/audit local media
  - Conduct focus panels to learn about community concerns
  - Interview key informants including potential non-attendees
  - Share your findings with your client and seek their feedback

- What type of programming can you incorporate in your municipal event to ensure that you represent every facet of the community as well as maintain a level of quality and professionalism throughout the program?
  - Survey the interests of your potential attendees and then audit the local resources available to match supply and demand
  - Appoint advisory panels representing underserved populations to help you produce an inclusive event
  - Hire professional talent directors to coach, produce, and present the local entertainment

- Why is the permanent full-time and part-time staff an important consideration at the venue where the event will be held? How can you raise the level of their performance without circumventing their existing training programs?
  - The staff, in fact, becomes the "cast" for the event and later become the "stars", once the opening events have concluded. Therefore, their skills and talents must be addressed and improved as part of the event design and planning process
  - Meet with the human resources director and determine how you can compliment and enhance their existing program

Good Luck, Grads!
- In planning for the luncheon next year, how can the university clearly identify who is in charge of planning the luncheon?
  - Identify the event manager and establish an organizational chart
  - Determine to whom the event manager reports
  - Establish a committee to select the student speaker

- What type of efficient organizational chart would you recommend for such an event in an academic environment?
  - A faculty committee should supervise the event manager
  - The event manager should supervise voluntary student committees

- What other techniques would be helpful to save, track, and retrieve in the event history?
    - A database of prospective and actual attendees
    - A time line that is updated at the end if the event
    - A production schedule that is updated at the end of the event

- How would you create a checklist for the various elements of the event?
    - A decision checklist should be created
    - A site inspection checklist should be created
    - A vendor checklist should be established

Show Me the Money!
- How would you prepare for to the meeting with your vendors?
    - Do your homework. Analyze why and how your cash shortfall occurred, what is required to cure this problem, and when it will be corrected
    - Use visuals and written reports to communicate this information

- What kind of research should be done before any financial contract negotiations?
    - Determine to the best of your ability the financial position of each of your vendors
    - Analyze the micro and macroeconomic conditions
    - Research your cash and credit position

- What incentive can organizers provide to sponsors and participants to generate cash?
    - Discounts for pre-payment may be offered
    - Additional benefits, such as VIP hospitality incentives for sponsors
    - VIP services for participants, such as reserves, special seating for planning sessions or special events

- What other solutions could organizers use to attract necessary funds?
    - Establish a line of credit with banks
    - Negotiate best terms with vendors to postpone payment without interest or penalties
    - Seek interest free short-term loans from members, lenders, or others

Homeland Security Alert: From Yellow to Orange

- Should the Event Leader have checked with officials (and if so, whom) in addition to the venue manager prior to formulating the code-orange plan? Yes, if possible, the Event Leader should have checked with the Department of Homeland Security or local Public Safety officials.
- What other questions should the Event Leader have asked in addition to those listed in the case study?
    - Is there a biological risk? Is there a trauma facility nearby with a safe room to isolate victims who have had biological weapons exposure?
- What could the Event leader have done in advance to anticipate a change in the threat level so that the event would have been prepared for this new development?
    - Close contact with the department of Homeland Security and local and state and provincial public safety officials may have provided early information to promote better preparedness.
- During the ingress for the event, what else could the Event Leader have done to satisfy his or her guests and increase the feeling of security and comfort?
    - The Event Leader could have added uniformed security guards to demonstrate a presence of control and command for the event.

SAMPLE
UNDERGRADUATE COURSE OUTLINE

Event Leadership

Course Outline

Instructor:	Dr. Joe Goldlblatt, CSEP
E-mail:	joe.goldblatt@temple.edu
	Note: E-mail is the preferred form of communication.
Address:	201B Vivacqua Hall (main campus)
Telephone:	(215) 204-9015
Office Hours:	Tuesdays-Thursdays 12pm-1:30pm, Thursdays 4:30pm-5:30pm, or by appointment.
Class hours:	Thursdays, 2:00pm-4:30pm
Class location:	Temple University City Center (TUCC) Room 406

Course Philosophy

Remember that life is a celebration or can be a celebration.
One of the most important things is to teach man how to celebrate.

Heschel, A. (*1959),* "Who Is Man", <u>Between God and Man</u> The Free Press: NY.

Course Description
This course is designed to provide a thorough overview of the meetings, conventions, and events industry. Topics will include the feasibility, viability and sustainability of the event process, the strategic planning, business development, marketing, human resource management, finance and budgeting, event creation and event orchestration, communications, and career development aspects of event leaders. This is a writing intensive course and will require writing competency in a number of written assignments.

Course Objectives
At the conclusion of the course students will be expected to:

1. Differentiate between event management and event leadership.
2. Conduct the strategic planning process for event development.
3. Promote effective strategic communications among event stakeholders.
4. Drive business results.
5. Plan and manage the financial and budgetary aspects of each event.
6. Develop and execute the human resources plan for the event.

7. Establish and implement the strategic marketing plan for the event.
8. Create the event.
9. Orchestrate the event.
10. Provide standard and customary ethical, legal, risk management, safety, and security analysis and management for the event.
11. Provide a comprehensive personal career plan.

Required Texts
Goldblatt, J. (2008), <u>Special Events: The Roots and Wings of Celebration, Fifth Edition</u>, John Wiley & Sons: New York, New York. (Available October September 2007).

Recommended Texts for Additional Reading
Goldblatt, J., Supovitz, F. (1999), <u>Dollars & Events, How to Succeed in the Special Events Business</u>, John Wiley & Sons: New York, NY.*

Goldblatt, Joe, Nelson, Kathleen (2000) <u>The International Dictionary of Event Management</u>, John Wiley & Sons, Inc.: New York, New York

Ernst and Young (1990), <u>The Complete Guide to Special Event Management,</u> John Wiley & Sons: New York, NY

Graham, S., Goldblatt, J. and Delpy, L. (1995), <u>The Ultimate Guide to Sport Event Management and Marketing</u>, Irwin Professional Publishing: Burr Ridge, IL.*

Hoyle, L. (2002) <u>Event Marketing</u>, John Wiley & Sons, Inc.: New York, NY.*

Lipton, B. (1995), <u>Barnett Lipton Collection</u>, Event Management and Marketing Archives.

Malouf, L. (1999), <u>Behind the Scenes at Special Events</u>, John Wiley & Sons: New York: NY.*

Morton, J. (1994), <u>Jack Morton Collection</u>, Event Management and Marketing Archives, Gelman Library, The George Washington University Department of Special Collections: Washington, DC.

Goldblatt, J., Nelson, K. (2001) <u>The International Dictionary of Event Management, Second Edition,</u> John Wiley & Sons, Inc.: New York, NY.*

Rutherford-Silvers, J. (2003) <u>Professional Event Coordination</u>, John Wiley & Sons Inc: New York, NY.*

Schaumann, P. (2004) <u>Successful Destination Management</u>, John Wiley & Sons Inc.: New York, NY.*

Skinner, B. (2002) <u>Event Sponsorship</u>, John Wiley & Sons, Inc.: New York, NY.*

Sonder, M. (2003) <u>Event Entertainment and Production,</u> John Wiley & Sons, Inc.: New York, NY.*

Supovitz, F. (2004) The <u>Sport Event Playbook</u>, John Wiley & Sons, Inc.: New York: NY.*

Tarlow, P. (2002) <u>Event Risk Management and Safety</u>, John Wiley & Sons, Inc.: New York, NY.*

Weirsma, B. (1994), <u>Creative Event Development,</u> Weirsma: Indianapolis, IN.

Class Policies on Evaluation

- **Respect for Andragogical Policy**

Students will demonstrate respect for the instructor and visiting speakers, as well as for one another in the classroom setting. Such respectful behavior includes constructive participation in scholarly discussion. Students are not expected to challenge an instructor's andragogical philosophy. For example, a student is encouraged to question why an economic principle is applied to this course, not why a project is only given a two-week preparation period or how or why an exam is constructed and written.

- **E-mail Etiquette**

The instructor will delete emails by students who do not use a Temple University account or who are not registered with the STHM Blackboard community. Email use does not relieve students of the responsibility of confirming the communication with the instructor. A timely email response will be subject to the instructor's commitment to research, scholarly activity, and service.

- **Classroom Conduct**

This course requires professional and respectful classroom conduct. Students engaging the following activities (including but not limited to): cell phone usage, inappropriate posture, reading other non-class materials, chatting and sleeping will be dismissed from that class meeting.

- **Make up Exams**

Will be evaluated at the instructor's sole discretion. Detailed instructions for all assignments will be provided. Students are expected to carefully follow these instructions.

- **Late Assignments**

Late assignments are not permitted. Late assignments will receive one lower grade for each day the assignment is late. Late papers will be not be accepted except for under exceptional circumstances and only if permission is granted by the instructor in advance in writing.

- **Grade Calculation**

Grades are based upon total accumulated points. The grade scale is included in the course outline.

- **Incompletes**

Incompletes are rarely given. "The notation of 'I' (incomplete) may be given by the instructor when a student has not completed the work of the course by the time the grades must be turned in, but has made a written agreement with the instructor" (Undergraduate Bulleting, Temple University). If reasons for unfinished work are acceptable to instructor, the incomplete work is small, and the student's standing in the course is satisfactory, an in complete will be given.

- **Presentation and Delivery/Transmission of Assignments**

All assignments must be typed. Points will be deducted for spelling, syntax, and grammatical errors. All referencing must be correct and accurate. Neatness and precision are essential in this course. Please use the Temple University Writing Center as required to complete your assignments: (www.temple.edu.writingctr/index.html).

- **Academic Integrity and Honesty**

Plagiarism (citations without attribution) and academic cheating is prohibited. "Plagiarism is the unacknowledged use of another person's ideas, another person's words, another person's assistance. Normally, all work done for courses is expected to be the individual effort of the student presenting the work. The penalty for academic dishonesty can vary from reprimand to a failing grade in the course to suspension or expulsion from the University." (Temple University Bulletin)

- **Doctrine of Individual Responsibility**

All students are expected to support the Doctrine of Individual Responsibility as adopted by the School.

- **Student and Faculty Academic Rights and Responsibilities**

Freedom to teach and freedom to learn are inseparable facets of academic freedom. The freedom to learn depends upon appropriate opportunities and conditions in the classroom, on the campus, and in the larger community. The University and the faculty have a responsibility to provide students with opportunities and protections that promote the learning process in all its aspects. Students similarly should exercise their freedom with responsibility. Temple University therefore reaffirms its commitment to academic freedom, and adopts the academic freedom principles applicable to faculty and students. You can find this information and policy at:
http://policies.temple.edu/getdoc.asp?policy_no=03.70.02

- **Prerequisites**

Students must conform to all prerequisites and admission requirements for this course.

- **Students responsibilities**

Promptness and punctuality is required for this course. **The instructor defines "on time" as "early."** Students shall arrive early whenever possible and always prepared for the assigned work. Students arriving late may not be admitted for the individual class session. No food or drink is allowed in class. Students must be prepared for each session. The material that is assigned should be read and analyzed prior to the session where it will be discussed. Students must be prepared to discuss and ask questions about the assigned reading material.

- **Grading**

A, A- Outstanding: Far surpasses the assignment requirements, well organized, analytical rather than descriptive, solid resources used where required, excellent in grammar, syntax, style and presentation.

B+, B, B- Very Good: Project exceeds the minimal requirements of the assignment, paper is well-organized, paper may be more descriptive than analytical-may not probe deeply to explain differences or contradictions, resources consulted not as extensive as the A paper, solid though not perfect grammar, syntax, style, and presentation.

C+, C, C- Average : Project may not meet all criteria of the assignment, organization and presentation are below average, paper is far too descriptive, few/and or inappropriate references are used, grammar, syntax, style, and presentation is poor, little effort is displayed.

D, F Below Average/Fail: Project does not meet the minimum criteria for acceptance.

- **Plagiarism and Academic cheating**

From the Temple University Undergraduate Bulletin:
http://www.temple.edu/bulletin/ugradbulletin/policies_part2.htm#pac
Temple University strongly believes in academic honesty and integrity. Plagiarism and academic cheating are, therefore, prohibited. Essential to intellectual growth is the development of independent thought and a respect for the thoughts of others. The prohibition against plagiarism and cheating is intended to foster this independence and respect.

Plagiarism is the unacknowledged use of another person's labor, another person's ideas, another person's words, and another person's assistance. Normally, all work done for courses -- papers, examinations, homework exercises, laboratory reports, oral presentations -- is expected to be the individual effort of the student presenting the work. Any assistance must be reported to the instructor. If the work has entailed consulting other resources – journals, books or other media – these resources must be cited in a manner appropriate for this course. It is the instructor's responsibility to indicate the appropriate manner of citation. Everything used from other sources – suggestions for organization of ideas, ideas themselves, or actual language – must be cited. **Failure to cite borrowed material constitutes plagiarism.**

Citation format:
(Books, Journals)
Goldblatt, J. (2008) Special Events: The Roots and Wings of Celebration, Fifth Edition, John Wiley & Sons, Inc: Hoboken, NJ.

(Personal interviews)
Smith, M. (2004) Personal interview.
(Internet)
www.ises.com (2004) Page title and number.

Academic cheating is, generally, the thwarting or breaking of the general rules of academic work or the specific rules of the individual courses. It includes falsifying data; submitting, without the instructor's approval, work in one course which was done for another; helping others to plagiarize or cheat from one's own or another's work; or actually doing the work of another person.

The penalty for academic dishonesty can vary from a reprimand and receiving a failing grade for a particular assignment, to a failing grade in the course, to suspension or expulsion from the University. The penalty varies with the nature of the offense, individual instructor, the department, and the school or college.

Students who believe that they have been unfairly accused may appeal through the school of college's academic grievance procedure. See <u>Grievances</u>.

Course Outcomes

As a result of this course students will understand the theoretical and practical foundations for effective twenty-first century event leadership. Furthermore, students will learn how to research, design, plan, coordinate, and evaluate professional events. At the conclusion of this course students will demonstrate general competence in the following areas:

Know: Recognize and use standard and customary event management terms.

Comprehend: Understand the purpose and value of developing a wide range of events.

Apply: Demonstrate through actual practice skills in planning and coordinating events based upon a case using an actual external agency.

Analyze: Critically analyze the sustainable events strengths, weaknesses, opportunities, and threats of events using the SWOT analysis.

Evaluate: Thoroughly evaluate the various elements involved in developing events.

Synthesize: Demonstrate ability to synthesize all event elements to effectively allocate scarce resources for maximum benefit.

Instructional Methods

Instructional methods will include but not be limited to lecture, debate, independent research, guest speakers, group discussion, practicum experience, completion of a professional event learning/career development portfolio. Graduate level students are required to complete an additional feasibility, viability, and sustainability plan for an event organization.

Assessment Methods

Students will be assessed using a wide range of methods including but not limited to tests, essays, oral presentations, written projects, and a learning/career development portfolio. For the capstone assessment, students will prepare a professional event learning/career development portfolio documenting the eleven components/duties/tasks of an event.

Curricular, Co-curricular and Extra-curricular Assignments

1. 1000 word essay comparing and contrasting three or more books from the canon of event management literature. <u>The essay must discuss your personal philosophy of event management and then compare your philosophy with that of others (authors).</u> The essay must conclude with a comprehensive analysis and listing of your potential event management career outcomes before and after the essay was written and demonstrates how your thinking has been influenced by the readings. Complete citations must accompany the essay. Students will meet individually with the professor to receive and discuss their graded paper. **Due: Session Three**

2. Completion of **four** one page individual papers and submission prior to the beginning of each class date as shown below in course schedule.
   <u>Format for weekly papers:</u>
   - A. Introduction/executive summary of main points.
   - B. Detailed examination of each main point with supportive citations.
   - C. Summary and conclusion of main points, distillation of ideas, analysis, and evaluation.
   - D. References (citations of at least three sources).

3. Interview two or more event professionals and compare and contrast their thinking regarding one of the following topics: "What skills, talents and experiences are needed to become a successful event leader?" "What do you believe are the greatest challenges facing event leaders in the next ten years?" Each report should also include a description of the biographical data of the interviewee (experience, education, title). The report should conclude with a analysis of the different views of each interviewee and a summation of your emerging thinking as a result of these interviews. Each paper shall not exceed 1000 words. **Due: Session Seven**

   Alternative to Assignment 3: You may work as a team and survey (written) a minimum of 100 persons attending a major event (boxing match, wedding) at The Legendary Blue Horizon regarding their expectations and perceptions of events at the venue. The survey should also collect minimum demographic data such as gender, income level, zip codes. All data must be analyzed using measures of central tendency and presented with graphs, charts, and written narrative. Note, if this alternative is selected the entire team will share the same grade for this project.

4. Attendance at one Greater Philadelphia International Special Events Society (ISES) or Professional Convention Management Association (PCMA) meeting. Provide a receipt to the instructor certifying your attendance. Submit a 300 word SWOT analysis (strengths, weaknesses, opportunities and threats) of the meeting/event with your receipt. **Due: At final examination.**

5. Participate as a volunteer during an event(s) for a minimum of 10 hours. Submit a letter from the event organizer certifying your participation. Submit a 300 word listing of the duties and tasks you performed as a volunteer. **Due: At final examination.**

6. Submit a strategic event development plan for The Legendary Blue Horizon venue as described below. The plan must address central challenges and opportunities of the Legendary Blue Horizon and provide concrete and specific recommendations based upon your group research. **Due: At final examination.**

Legendary Blue Horizon Strategic Plan Components:
1. Table of contents
2. Executive summary describing history and scope of the Legendary Blue Horizon (number of years, number of attendees, volunteers, budget, location, public/private perception, etc).
3. Describe the challenges and opportunities related to the Legendary Blue Horizon and provide analysis based from the course to make recommendations to improve this process and outcome.
4. Describe how the event strategic plan will <u>drives business results for the Legendary Blue Horizon</u>. What are the business outcomes from your plan? Provide concrete, specific, and measurable recommendations to improve the business results. The recommendations should be the result of your research of other comparable best practice organizations as evidenced in the literature and through interviews.
5. Analyze the strategic marketing plan for the Legendary Blue Horizon and provide recommendations to promote a higher yield in the future based upon concepts learned in the course and from other sources.
6. Analyze the human resources plan for the Legendary Blue Horizon and provide recommendations based upon concepts learned in the course and from other sources. Include current (if available) and recommended organizational chart.
7. Analyze the financial and budget plan and performance for the Legendary Blue Horizon and make recommendations for improvement

based upon concepts learned in the course and from other sources. Include current (if available) and recommended budget.

8. Describe the process used for creating events and make recommendations for improvement based upon concepts learned in the course and from other sources. Include current (if available) and recommended time line.

9. Analyze the ethical, legal, risk management, safety and security issues associated with planning and managing the events and provide recommendations for improving these outcomes based upon concepts learned in the course and from other sources.

10. Describe the process for orchestrating the events and provide recommendations for improvement based upon concepts learned in the course and from other sources. Include current (if available) and recommended production schedule.

11. Analyze your individual career development process, list any current learning gaps and describe the opportunities you will seize for closing these gaps with future learning experiences. Put your individual name on this document.

12. Summarize your individual learning outcomes from this project and class and describe how you will apply these outcomes to the leadership of future events. Put your individual name on this document.

13. References/citations for all materials cited.

14. Appendices: Examples of event literature such as photographs, invitations, videos, advertisements, public relations, and brochures.

Length and Format

Each section shall not exceed 300 words (approximately one page). Final project shall be submitted in a three ring binder with cover page and tabs separating each section.

Course sessions, dates, topics, guest speakers (tentative), competencies, assignments, readings, and assignment due dates (Subject to change by instructor due to availability of guest speakers).

Week One:
Lecture: Welcome to the Excitement Industry!
Distribution of syllabus.
Reading for next session: Chapter one and Case Study Number One.

Week Two:
Note: Class will meet at the Legendary Blue Horizon, 1314 North Broad Street, Philadelphia, PA.
Lecture: Chapter One, Needs Assessment, Strategic Facility Audit.
Reading for next session: Complete chapter two and case study two.

Week Three:
Guest speaker: Sir Thomas Ingilby, Baronet, Ripley Castle, Great Britain
(www.ripleycastle.co.uk)
Lecture: Chapter Two, Models of Global Event Management
Reading for next session: Complete chapter three.
Assignment due: 1000 word essay.

Week Four:
Lecture: Chapter four, Developing and Implementing the Event Plan
Reading for next session: Complete chapter five and case study number five.
Assignment due: Submit draft of time line and production schedule for your event.

Week Five:
Note: Class will meet at the Pennsylvania Convention Center, 1101 Arch Street.
Lecture: Chapter five.
Reading for next session: Complete chapter six and case study six.

Week Six:
Lecture: Chapter six.
Reading for next session: Chapter seven and case study seven.
Assignment due: Interview essay due.

Week Seven:
Lecture: Chapter seven
Reading for next session: Complete chapter eight and case study eight.
Assignment due: Submit draft budget with account codes.
Mid term Examination covering chapters 1-5: Multiple choice and essay.

Week Eight:
Lecture: Chapter eight.
Reading for next session: Complete chapter nine.

Week Nine:
Note: Class will meet at the National Constitution Center, 525 Arch Street.
Lecture: Chapter nine.
Reading for next session: Complete chapter ten and eleven.
Assignment due: Submit organizational chart using Microsoft Organizational Chart. Describe role and scope of each position.

Week Ten:
Lecture: Chapters ten and eleven.
Reading for next session: Complete chapters eleven and twelve.

Week Eleven:
Lecture: Chapter eleven and twelve.
Reading for next session: Complete chapter thirteen.
Assignment due: Use the Internet to research the history of *Super Bowl Half Time Spectacular* and be prepared to debate pro or con the following argument: Resolve the NFL Super Bowl Half Time Spectacular is No Longer Relevant and Should be Eliminated.

Week Twelve:
Lecture: Chapter thirteen.
The Great Debate: The class will be divided into two teams and you will argue for or against the resolution regarding the relevancy of the *Super Bowl Half Time Spectacular.*
Reading for next session: Complete chapter fourteen.
Assignment due: Submit comprehensive risk assessment, analysis, planning, and management strategy.

Week Thirteen:
Lecture: Chapter thirteen and final review.
Assignment due: Prepare for final presentations.

Note: All written work must be handed in at time of final examination.
(I)= Points based upon individual effort.
(G)=Points based upon group effort

Basis of Grade
1. 100 word Topical essay

Research	5
Quality of arguments	3
Spelling, grammar, construction	2
Sub total	10 (I)

2. One page weekly papers

Research	5
Spelling, grammar, construction	5
Sub total	10 (four at 2.5 points each) (I)

3. Interview essay (See alternative assignment above)

Quality of interview questions	5
Analysis of responses	3
Spelling, grammar, construction	2
Sub total	10 (I)

4. Meeting attendance	5 (I)
5. Experiential learning (volunteer activities)	5 (I)
6. Mid term examination	15 (I)
7. Debate and class participation	5 (I)

8. Event and career portfolio

Adherence to instruction	3
Analysis	1
Evaluation	2
Research	5
References	1
Spelling, grammar, construction	1
Team evaluation	2 (I)
Sub total	15 (G)

9. Final examination

Multiple choice	10
Essay	10
Subtotal	20 (I)

10. Class participation	5
Total possible points	**100**

Grading scale
A: 93 and above
A-: 92-90
B+: 89-87
B: 86-83
B-: 82-80
C+: 79-77
C: 76-73
C-: 72-70
D+: 69-67
D: 66-63
D-: 62-60
F 59 and below

Note: Instructor may alter syllabus at anytime with advance written notice to students. Guest speakers and site visits subject to change with advance written notice to students.

Appendix 2
Sample Chapter Test Questions

Multiple Choice Questions

CHAPTER ONE
1. The director of public relations at Disneyland first defined the phrase "special events" as:
   - A. Entertainment
   - B. Programming
   - C. Diversion
   - D. "That which is different from a normal day of living."

2. The term *event* is derived from the Latin term *evenire* that means:
   - A. Outcome
   - B. Results
   - C. Ending
   - D. Beginning

3. According to the International Association of Amusement Parks (IAAPA) and Attractions, over 50 percent of the baby boomers have:
   - A. Cars
   - B. Discretionary income
   - C. Homes
   - D. Technology

4. One market that you may wish to target for your event, is entitled the:
   - A. Gray panthers
   - B. Adventurists
   - C. Wanderlust singletons
   - D. Millenials

5. A major psychographic change that affects events is entitled:
   - A. Tribing
   - B. Adventuring
   - C. Probing
   - D. Exploring

6. All professions are represented by all of the following unique characteristics, except:
   - A. A unique body of knowledge
   - B. *A president, vice president, secretary, and treasurer.*
   - C. Voluntary standards that result in certification.
   - D. Accepted code of ethics.

7. The latin term *celebro* means:
    A. To honor.
    B. To perform.
    C. To ritualize.
    D. All of the above.

8. Event Leadership sub fields include all of the following, except:
    A. Civic events
    B. Fairs and festivals
    C. Social-life cycle events
    D. Ice cream events

9. Event Leadership financial success requires that you achieve all of the following, except:
    A. Borrow lots of money.
    B. Seek professional counsel.
    C. Identify and use efficient financial technology.
    D. Control overhead and build wealth.

10. Peter Kagwa believes that:
    A. History is unimportant.
    B. Focus only upon today and tomorrow.
    C. To know where you are going, it is important to know where you have come from.
    D. Wings are more important than roots.

CHAPTER TWO

1. The five phases in the Event Leadership process include:
    A. Research and design
    B. Planning and coordination and evaluation
    C. None of these
    D. A&B

2. The first phase in the Event leadership process is:
    A. Design
    B. Planning
    C. Research
    D. Evaluation

3. Evaluation is directly connected to:
    A. Research
    B. Evaluation
    C. Design
    D. Planning

4. Event managers primarily use quantitative research to determine demographic information such as:
    A. Lifestyles
    B. Attitudes
    C. Values
    D. Age, gender, and income

5. One type of qualitative event management research includes conducting:
    A. Surveys
    B. Focus groups
    C. Intercept interviews
    D. None of the above

6. It is best to use:
    A. Both quantitative and qualitative research
    B. Only quantitative research
    C. Only qualitative research
    D. Ethnocentric Pearson's Profiles

7. Your Event Leadership research should be:
    A. Highly valid
    B. Highly reliable
    C. Highly favorable
    D. A&B

8. When selecting the appropriate pre-event research method for examining the culture of the local community where the event will occur you may wish to:
    A. Collect only demographic data
    B. Collect only psychographic data
    C. A&B
    D. Use participant/Observer techniques

9. The term EMBOK means:
    A. Event Management Body of Knowledge
    B. Event Motor Becomes King
    C. Electrical Management Business Knowledge
    D. Environmental Management Body of Knowledge

10. Jean McFaddin recommends that Event Leaders prepare for inclement weather by:
    A. Having a contingency plan.
    B. Communicating the contingency plan to others.
    C. Washing your car in advance.
    D. A & B

CHAPTER THREE

1. Research (data) + design =
   A. Planned successful outcomes.
   B. Fewer risks.
   C. Greater opportunities.
   D. Increased profits.

2. The senses involved in the five-card draw are all of the following except:
   A. Smell
   B. Visual
   C. Sensualization
   D. Tactile

3. If you are designing a event for a corporation that wishes to promote guest recall of the company logo, the predominate sense should be:
   A. Visual
   B. Smell
   C. Tactile
   D. Auditory

4. If your event has 3000 square feet/meters of available dance floor how many persons may be accommodated for dancing?
   A. 500
   B. 200
   C. 400
   D. 300

5. If a guest arrives without a invitation they should be directed to the:
   A. Office
   B. Courtesy table
   C. Back room
   D. None of the above

6. To improve audience sight lines and encourage greater interaction between speaker and audience members:
   A. Curve the chairs for optimum theater or classroom style set up
   B. Straighten the chairs for better viewing
   C. Stagger the chairs for clearer views
   D. Add seat cushions.

7. When designing a parade float you should consider all of the following except:
    A. What does the parade committee or organization allow in terms of size, materials, and thematic design?
    B. Under what meteorological conditions and in what climate will the float be used.
    C. Will the float appear on television.
    D. How many pot holes appear per block

8. The vertical pedestal that holds a flower arrangement in the center of the banquet table is referred to by florists as a:
    A. Stick
    B. Upright stand
    C. Lifter
    D. Epergne

9. The appropriate décor, entertainment, and food/beverages for a Mardi Gras theme party may be:
    A. Purple, green, and blue balloons, an accordion player, and spaghetti Alfredo
    B. Red, white, and gold balloons, a rock band, and French cuisine
    C. Purple, green, and gold balloons, a jazz band, and Creole cuisine
    D. None of the above

10. Jay Downie designs festivals so that the event becomes:
    A. The focus.
    B. The secondary consideration.
    C. The environment.
    D. None of the above.

CHAPTER FOUR

1. One major difference between corporate events and those funded by the use of not for profit organizations is the use of:
   A. Full time staff
   B. Temporary help
   C. Leaders
   D. Volunteers

2. To encourage volunteers to continue to support your event you must include:
   A. Rewards
   B. Cash
   C. Free use of cars
   D. None of the above

3. The Event Leader should appear at the center or near the top of the:
   A. Ledger
   B. Budget
   C. Organizational chart
   D. Command center

4. A bottom up organizational chart is primarily used to depict:
   A. Extremely rigid organizations
   B. Volunteer organizations
   C. Military organizations
   D. Sophisticated corporate organizations

5. Every event organization should have:
   A. Written policies and procedures
   B. Scale models
   C. Life drawings
   D. Medical screenings

6. Procedures are:
   A. Conceived and approved by the organizations trustees
   B. The implementation tactics for policy.
   C. Not essential
   D. None of the above

7. The more efficient you are in your time management the more:
   A. The less likely you will be to run overtime
   B. The more likely you will be to finish your tasks early
   C. The more projects you manage will be completed
   D. All of the above

8. All volunteers must be:
    A. Trained
    B. Experienced
    C. Quick
    D. Personable

9. Josh McCall believes that in the age of experiential event marketing, the foundation of his firms success is:
    A. Consumer engagement with the product or service
    B. Data
    C. Promotion
    D. None of the above

10. Sheila Graham urges people interested in entering the special events profession to:
    A. Find a web site
    B. Find a mentor
    C. Find a teacher
    D. Find a book

CHAPTER FIVE
1. The financial philosophy for your event may be:
   A. Profit oriented
   B. Break-even
   C. Loss leader or hosted
   D. All of the above

2. When conducting research for your event review the:
   A. General economy
   B. Local rumors
   C. Reasonable projected income
   D. A & C

3. Typical income categories for your event may be:
   A. Payments to sub contractors
   B. Sponsorship
   C. Registration fees
   D. B & C

4. All of the following are typical expenses for your event, except:
   A. Merchandise sales income
   B. Advertising
   C. Audiovisual equipment and services
   D. Entertainment

5. Make certain that your accounting software is compatible with your:
   A. Lawyer
   B. Banker
   C. Accountant
   D. Caterer

6. Fixed overhead expenses for your event include the following items, except:
   A. Rent
   B. Telephone
   C. Catering for meal functions
   D. Insurance

7. Variable expenses include:
   A. Catering
   B. Audio visual
   C. Registration materials
   D. All of the above

8. The difference between net and gross profit for your event is the:
    A. Type of software you use
    B. Percentage of fixed overhead expenses that was dedicated to producing a specific event
    C. The staff salaries
    D. The benefits

9. The foreign exchange rate is the:
    A. Price of one currency expressed in another currency
    B. The Euro
    C. The amount set by the Federal Reserve
    D. None of the above

10. Frank Supovitz states that one responsibility of an Event Leader is to:
    A. Establish sufficient revenues
    B. Under report earnings
    C. Respond to economic pressures
    D. A & C

CHAPTER SIX

1. The most common methods of identifying and managing appropriate resources for your event include:
   A. Conduct a needs assessment
   B. Distribute request for proposal
   C. Monitor contract performance
   D. All of the above

2. Vendors for your event may include:
   A. Advertising agencies
   B. Audio visual providers
   C. Government lawyers
   D. A&B

3. There are three types of caterers who may include:
   A. Institutional
   B. Off premise
   C. Concessionaire
   D. All of the above

4. Caterers may require:
   A. Utilities
   B. Grass
   C. Water
   D. A&C

5. The type of service style where guests remain standing is the:
   A. Buffet
   B. Standing reception
   C. French
   D. Russian

6. The average length of time for a cocktail reception is:
   A. Two hours
   B. One and a half hours
   C. Thirty minutes to one hour
   D. Fifteen minutes

7. The production schedule begins with:
   A. Load-in
   B. Clean up
   C. Electric hook ups
   D. Water sourcing

8. All of the following are typical operational conflicts, except for:
   A. Speaker or entertainer cancels
   B. Multiple vendors arriving simultaneously
   C. Caterer becomes ill in the kitchen
   D. Late-arriving vendors

9. When a speaker or entertainer cancels you may wish to:
   A. Tell the guests there is a big problem
   B. Lead a sing along
   C. Turn off the lights
   D. Use taped music or pre-taped video to cover.

10. Mary Jordan advises us to:
    A. Emulate the habits of successful people
    B. Stay true to yourself
    C. Never burn bridges
    D. All of the above

CHAPTER SEVEN
1. The key informants who will contribute to the production schedule include:
   A. Admissions coordinator
   B. Caterer
   C. Fire department
   D. All of the above

2. To make certain the production schedule remains consistent and "on schedule" you should appoint several:
   A. Monitors
   B. Volunteers
   C. CEO's
   D. CFO's

3. When handling a change during the event you should issue a written:
   A. Cease and desist notice
   B. Stop, look, and listen bulletin
   C. Change notice
   D. None of the above

4. Meeting event managers refer to the production schedule as the:
   A. Event Specification Guide (APEX)
   B. Staffing list
   C. Production outlook
   D. Manifest

5. The term LED means:
   A. Light emitting diode
   B. Light energy display
   C. Longitudinal energy diode
   D. None of the above

6. One of the key issues the caterer must control is:
   A. Location
   B. Size of guests
   C. Size of tables
   D. Height of chairs

7. For a brief networking breakfast, the preferred catering service style is:
   A. French service
   B. Seated banquet
   C. Passed items
   D. Standing buffet

8. The ellipsoidal spotlight is designed to accept a:
   - A. Computer chip
   - B. Gobo
   - C. Gel
   - D. B & C

9. Soundscaping typically consists of:
   - A. Voices from throughout the room speaking at once
   - B. Small horns broadcasting music from overhead
   - C. Miniature speakers throughout the venue creating different moods and atmospheres through recorded sound effects and music
   - D. Huge speakers in all four corners

10. In addition to the U.S. Fourth of July celebration, Zambelli fireworks has seen huge growth for:
    - A. Weddings
    - B. Private birthdays
    - C. New Years Eve
    - D. A&C

CHAPTER EIGHT
1. The five P's in marketing are:
   A. Product, Promotion, Price, Public Relations, and Place
   B. Promotion, Price, Place, Position, and Punctuation
   C. Price, Place, Promotion, Principle, and Pronouncement
   D. None of the above

2. Every event product should incorporate:
   A. Free things
   B. Added value
   C. Cheap tickets
   D. None of the above

3. Promotion may include all of the following except:
   A. Advertising
   B. Stunts
   C. Trickery
   D. Cross promotions

4. The two factors that determine price are:
   A. The financial philosophy of the organization/event and competition
   B. The color of the tickets and the location
   C. The location and the date
   D. The salaries of the event manager and his or her assistant

5. Advertising is what you say about your event, whereas public relations is:
   A. You permit to be said about your event on the radio
   B. You permit to be said about your event on the television
   C. Others say about your event
   D. None of the above

6. Place not only implies the taste or style of the event, it also defines the:
   A. Caterer
   B. Decorator
   C. Pyrotechnician
   D. Location of the event

7. An example of external/internal event marketing is a:
   A. Retail event held in a shopping center
   B. Conference
   C. Exhibition
   D. Trade show

8. When launching a new product the event marketer should first:
   A. Find out how much the client will spend
   B. Identify the location
   C. Choose the caterer
   D. Determine the goals and objectives of the product launch event

9. The event invitation should include the:
   A. Name of host or event organizer
   B. Date, time, and location
   C. Dress requirements
   D. All of the above

10. One of the things David Rich looks for in hiring new staff is:
    A. Proper dress
    B. An unquenchable thirst for knowing how things work
    C. Linguistic ability
    D. Cash handling ability

CHAPTER NINE

1. The Internet is a major opportunity for expanding your events:
   - A. Brand
   - B. Sales
   - C. Communication ability
   - D. All of the above

2. One of the problems with on line sales is:
   - A. Guaranteeing security for the purchaser
   - B. Low power
   - C. Narrow band versus broad band
   - D. Dial up

3. Your web site can provide customer support if it provides:
   - A. Color graphics
   - B. Line drawings
   - C. FAQ's
   - D. None of the above

4. You may conduct market testing by using a:
   - A. Chat room
   - B. Photo gallery
   - C. Check list
   - D. Grocery cart

5. A blog is a:
   - A. Listing of random thoughts
   - B. Web log of comments
   - C. Error on your web page
   - D. Virus in your computer

6. A podcast is a:
   - A. Downloadable video or audio telecast on the Internet
   - B. Broadcast under a large pod at a festival
   - C. Satellite in outer space that pods the message to the event
   - D. None of the above

7. RFID means:
   - A. Radio Fast Interface Display
   - B. Radio Frequency Identification
   - C. Redial Forum Interpretation
   - D. Residual Frequency Identification

8. Event Leaders use RFID to:
    A. Track the attendance of participants
    B. Talk to computers
    C. Teach technology
    D. Telecommute from home

9. An emerging electronic consumer generated marketing form is:
    A. Ear implants
    B. Wrist watches
    C. Cellular phone text messaging
    D. Dental radio implants

10. According to Dessislava Boshnakova, every day in Bulgaria they are:
    A. Seeing 100 percent growth in the number of wedding planners
    B. Creating new rituals from their history
    C. Paying for professional event consultation
    D. All of the above.

CHAPTER TEN

1. The four essential parts of a contract are:
   - A. Parties and offer
   - B. Consideration and acceptance
   - C. Liability, Insurance, Cancellation, and Indemnity
   - D. A & B

2. A safe event environment implies that it is:
   - A. Somewhat safe
   - B. Primarily safe
   - C. Free from hazards
   - D. None of the above

3. A secure event environment is one that is:
   - A. Somewhat protected
   - B. Completely protected
   - C. Clean
   - D. Protected from future harm

4. The legal, ethical, and safety-security aspects of your event can affect :
   - A. The Insurance premium
   - B. Licensure
   - C. Bottom line financial results
   - D. None of the above

5. Additional contract terms include all of the following, except:
   - A. Terms
   - B. Cancellation
   - C. Force majeure (Act of God)
   - D. Spelling

6. To play music at your live commercial event you must first have a license from:
   - A. ASCAP
   - B. BMI
   - C. A and / or B
   - D. None of the above

7. A risk assessment meeting could involve:
   - A. Admissions manager
   - B. Catering manager
   - C. Electrician
   - D. All of the above

8. During the pre-event inspection you should confirm that:
    A. Accreditation systems are in working order
    B. Admissions personnel are in place
    C. Doors are working properly in case of evacuation
    D. All of the above

9. Typical event insurance products include all of the following except:
    A. Comprehensive General Liability (CGL)
    B. Cancellation
    C. Automobile
    D. Furious guest

10. According to April Harris, Event Leaders in higher education may earn:
    A. Under $20,000 annually
    B. Over $100,000 annually
    C. From $23,000 to over $60,000 annually
    D. None of the above

CHAPTER ELEVEN

1. Ethics are:
   A. Moral actions
   B. Legally binding
   C. Actions by individuals or groups based on the business culture that is accepted at the time of the action
   D. None of the above

2. Common ethical problems within the events industry include:
   A. Gifts versus bribes
   B. Sexual harassment
   C. Staff members soliciting clients from previous employment at new place of employment
   D. All of the above

3. When Johnson & Johnson made their decisions after the Tylenol incident these decisions were based upon their:
   A. Legal opinion
   B. Credo
   C. Business plan
   D. Annual report

4. To avoid the ethical issue of theft of ideas by clients and competitors you could:
   A. Insert a copyright statement on proposals and notify others of infringement
   B. Sue them
   C. Call the news media
   D. None of the above

5. To avoid the ethical problem of your vendors accepting work directly from your clients you could:
   A. Warn them
   B. Threaten them
   C. Establish written policies
   D. Sue them

6. One way to avoid potential ethical problems is to review the:
   A. Legal code
   B. Bar code
   C. Directives from below
   D. Industry code of ethics (ISES)

7. To avoid the problem of accepting expensive gifts from vendors or those who wish to solicit your business you may:
    A. Ban or set a limit on gifts
    B. Only receive gifts from one vendor
    C. Only receive gifts from one store
    D. None of the above

8. Every event organization should have a:
    A. Internal code of ethics or procedures related to ethical issues
    B. High priced attorney
    C. Federal prosecutor
    D. All of the above

9. To avoid making complex ethical decisions in a vacuum or in isolation you may wish to appoint a:
    A. Ethics czar
    B. Ethical brain trust
    C. Minister
    D. Counselor

10. According to Zeren Earls, today, First Night new years eve, are held annually with:
    A. 150 celebrations worldwide
    B. 25 celebrations worldwide
    C. 10 celebrations worldwide
    D. None of the above

CHAPTER TWELVE

1. The major tasks of the technology and information system in Event Leadership is to:
    A. Collect, store and provide data to different levels of users
    B. Retrieve data
    C. Manage information
    D. Secure data

2. In batch data processing systems, event transactions are:
    A. Accumulated and processed individually
    B. Processed by sequence
    C. Accumulated and processed in groups
    D. Accumulated and discarded

3. In a real-time data processing system, transactions are entered as they:
    A. Occur
    B. Develop
    C. Delete
    D. Enter

4. Time sharing occurs when a system:
    A. Schedules minute time bands
    B. Services more than one branch of a event management company at the same time
    C. Cooperates with vendors
    D. None of the above

5. Three basic types of hardware configuration that are common in the event management industry are:
    A. September, March, and April analogs
    B. Annual, Semi annual, and Quarterly
    C. Online systems, PC systems, and distributed data processing
    D. None of the above

6. In a Electronic Data Interchange (EDI) system documents such as purchase orders, invoices, attendance projections, and checks are converted into standard form, permitting other companies to:
    A. Secure them
    B. Read and accept them
    C. File them
    D. Delete them

7. To prevent unauthorized use and alteration of files and data, access must be limited through:
   A. Passwords
   B. Handcuffs
   C. Iris scanners
   D. Fingerprints

8. The two major criteria that distinguish a data base are:
   A. Number of resources and search features
   B. Problems and solutions
   C. Challenges and Opportunities
   D. Nexis and Lexis

9. One major trend in event management technology is:
   A. Reduction in cost due to competition
   B. Increase in cost
   C. Instability
   D. None of the above

10. According to Steven Wood Schmader, Event leaders should:
    A. Network
    B. Nourish friendships
    C. Be committed to do whatever it takes to accomplish their goals
    D. All of the above

CHAPTER THIRTEEN
1. One of the primary keys to advancing your career in event management is:
    A. Networking
    B. Education
    C. Narrow experience
    D. None of the above

2. The four areas central to the profession of event management are:
    A. Creativity, Reliability, Dependability, and Facility management
    B. Punctuation, Communications, Coordination, Management
    C. Administration, Coordination, Marketing, and Risk management
    D. Selection, Negotiation, Construction, and de-construction

3. To succeed in the long term in this field you must:
    A. Cultivate experience
    B. Continue your industry education
    C. Maintain a positive attitude
    D. Excellent eye sight

4. In addition to education, successful event managers must have substantial:
    A. Relevant experience
    B. Contacts
    C. Favors from friends
    D. Vendors

5. To find a internship or externship you may wish to:
    A. Enroll in a educational program to receive help from a instructor with strong contacts
    B. Look in the phone book
    C. Ask friends
    D. None of the above

6. To become a Certified Special Events Professional (CSEP) you should first:
    A. Sit for the test
    B. Enroll in the program
    C. Begin studying
    D. Memorize 3000 terms

7. Finding a great job in the field of event management is a combination of:
    A. Timing, persistence, and talent
    B. Tenacity, temperament, and tediousness
    C. Toughness, elasticity, and uniqueness
    D. None of the above

8. Prior to sending out your resume you should send a:
    A. Business card
    B. E-mail
    C. Query letter
    D. All of the above

9. Your resume should describe the:
    A. Types of events you have coordinated or managed
    B. The number of attendees at each event
    C. The size of the budget of each event
    D. All of the above

10. Both Lucky Morimoto and Jen Kawamura acknowledge that the event industry is a:
    A. Laborious exercise
    B. Unfulfilling career
    C. Team effort
    D. Individual activity

Answer Key

Ch. 1
1. D	2. A	3. B	4. C	5. B
6. B	7. D	8. D	9. A	10. C

Ch. 2
1. D	2. C	3. A	4. D	5. B
6. A	7. D	8. D	9. A	10. D

Ch. 3
1. A	2. C	3. A	4. D	5. B
6. A	7. D	8. D	9. C	10. C

Ch. 4
1. D	2. A	3. C	4. B	5. A
6. B	7. D	8. A	9. A	10. B

Ch. 5
1. D	2. D	3. D	4. A	5. C
6. C	7. D	8. B	9. A	10. D

Ch. 6
1. D	2. D	3. D	4. D	5. B
6. C	7. A	8. C	9. D	10. D

Ch. 7
1. D	2. A	3. C	4. A	5. A
6. A	7. D	8. D	9. C	10. D

Ch. 8
1. A	2. B	3. C	4. A	5. C
6. D	7. A	8. D	9. D	10. B

Ch. 9
1. D	2. A	3. C	4. A	5. B
6. A	7. B	8. A	9. C	10. D

Ch. 10
1. D	2. C	3. D	4. C	5. D
6. C	7. D	8. D	9. D	10. C

Ch. 11
1. C	2. D	3. B	4. A	5. C
6. D	7. A	8. A	9. B	10. A

Ch. 12
1. A	2. C	3. A	4. B	5. C
6. B	7. A	8. A	9. A	10. D

Ch. 13
1. B	2. C	3. B	4. A	5. A
6. B	7. A	8. C	9. D	10. C

APPENDIX 3
Additional Resources

The Event Management and Marketing Archives
The George Washington University
Melvin Gelman Library
Department of Special Collections
www.gwu.edu/gelman

International Special Events Society
www.ises.com

Council for Hotel, Restaurant, Institution Education (CHRIE)
Convention Educators Special Interest Group
www.chrie.org

Meeting Professionals International
Listing of Education Programs in Event and Meeting Management
www.mpinet.org

Professional Convention Management Association
Body of Knowledge in Event Leadership
www.pcma.org

Printed in the United States
121681LV00001B/135-136/P

9 780470 135068